CAMBRIDGE LIBRARY COLLECTION

Books of enduring scholarly value

History

The books reissued in this series include accounts of historical events and movements by eye-witnesses and contemporaries, as well as landmark studies that assembled significant source materials or developed new historiographical methods. The series includes work in social, political and military history on a wide range of periods and regions, giving modern scholars ready access to influential publications of the past.

Note on the Historical Results Deducible From Recent Discoveries in Afghanistan

Henry T. Prinsep (1792–1878) was the son of a prominent East India Company servant, and like his father, Prinsep also spent much of his life in the East. He left Britain for Calcutta in 1809, at the age of seventeen, and stayed in India, working in a variety of roles, until his retirement in 1843. His brother James also lived in India and was a prominent scholar. Upon the latter's death in 1840, Prinsep found himself in possession of his brother's coin collection and a notebook, which became the basis of this work, published in 1844. Prinsep explains that the coins – which have inscriptions in both Greek and unknown languages – are valuable evidence of Alexander the Great's famous expedition to the east in the fourth century BCE. Prinsep also includes extensive illustrations of the coins, offering a fascinating view of an important archaeological discovery.

Cambridge University Press has long been a pioneer in the reissuing of out-of-print titles from its own backlist, producing digital reprints of books that are still sought after by scholars and students but could not be reprinted economically using traditional technology. The Cambridge Library Collection extends this activity to a wider range of books which are still of importance to researchers and professionals, either for the source material they contain, or as landmarks in the history of their academic discipline.

Drawing from the world-renowned collections in the Cambridge University Library, and guided by the advice of experts in each subject area, Cambridge University Press is using state-of-the-art scanning machines in its own Printing House to capture the content of each book selected for inclusion. The files are processed to give a consistently clear, crisp image, and the books finished to the high quality standard for which the Press is recognised around the world. The latest print-on-demand technology ensures that the books will remain available indefinitely, and that orders for single or multiple copies can quickly be supplied.

The Cambridge Library Collection will bring back to life books of enduring scholarly value (including out-of-copyright works originally issued by other publishers) across a wide range of disciplines in the humanities and social sciences and in science and technology.

Note on the Historical Results Deducible From Recent Discoveries in Afghanistan

HENRY THOBY PRINSEP

CAMBRIDGE
UNIVERSITY PRESS

CAMBRIDGE UNIVERSITY PRESS

Cambridge, New York, Melbourne, Madrid, Cape Town,
Singapore, São Paolo, Delhi, Tokyo, Mexico City

Published in the United States of America by Cambridge University Press, New York

www.cambridge.org
Information on this title: www.cambridge.org/9781108028714

© in this compilation Cambridge University Press 2011

This edition first published 1844
This digitally printed version 2011

ISBN 978-1-108-02871-4 Paperback

NOTE ON THE

HISTORICAL RESULTS,

DEDUCIBLE FROM RECENT

DISCOVERIES IN AFGHANISTAN.

BY

H. T. PRINSEP, Esq.

———

LONDON:

Wm. H. ALLEN AND CO.,

7, LEADENHALL STREET.

———

1844.

PREFACE.

THE Public are not unacquainted with the fact, that discoveries of much interest have recently been made in the
regions of Central Asia, which were the seat of Greek dominion for some hundred years after their conquest by Alexander. These discoveries are principally, but not entirely,
numismatic, and have revealed the names of sovereigns of
Greek race, and of their Scythian, and Parthian successors,
of none of whom is any mention to be found in the
extant histories of the East or West. There has also
been opened to the curious, through these coins, a language, the existence of which was hitherto unknown,
and which must have been the vernacular dialect of
some of the regions in which the Grecian colonies
were established. The coins possess particular value as a
key for the cypher of this language through their bilingual
legends and superscriptions, and have been extensively
and successfully used for that purpose. But the investigation deserves, and requires to be further prosecuted, for
there are inscriptions forthcoming in the language, which,
if the ingenuity of the learned should succeed in completely translating and explaining them, cannot fail to
throw much light, on the worse than Cimmerian darkness,
that still envelops the age and country which have be-
queathed them to us.

Amongst the earliest of those who directed public attention to these bilingual coins, and the most successful interpreter of their legends, was the late Mr. James Prinsep, Secretary of the Asiatic Society of Calcutta, and Editor of the Society's Journal, published monthly in that city. In both capacities he was naturally placed in direct and constant communication with those engaged in the work of practical discovery; and the assistance and instruction he was thus enabled to give, and readily and freely imparted to those, who, by the accident of position, were led to prosecute such researches, or who, by other means, became possessed of objects of antiquarian curiosity, was so frequently acknowledged by the gift of the articles discovered, that a very rich and extensive cabinet was the fruit. As an instance of the oriental liberality with which these things were presented, it may be stated, that, consequently upon a favorable mention in the Journal, of Gen. Ventura's researches at Manikyala, the vases, coins, and relics, found in the tope opened there in 1830, were freely and gratuitously given to the Editor by the General, and duplicates of his large assortment of Greco-Bactrian coins were similarly presented, in consideration of some little pains bestowed on the reading and classification of the more complete set, which the General made up to be forwarded to France.

Mr. James Prinsep, unfortunately, died before the investigation into the results of these discoveries had reached that point, which would warrant a satisfactory

classification and arrangement of the articles he so obtained. The cabinet thus came to his widow, rich and
various, but unsorted, and uncatalogued. In this condition, she applied to the Author of the following pages
for advice and assistance as to its disposal; and he in
consequence, as well as from a sense of duty, as for an
agreeable and profitable occupation, undertook its arrangement, referring for that purpose to modern works written
on the subject, and seeking in history, and in classic
literature, for information regarding the period to which
the coins and relics belonged.

Along with the cabinet, the note-book of the deceased
was placed in the Author's hands; and it is the possession
of that, and of the plates prepared originally for the
Journal, and still fortunately preserved, that has led the
Author to think, that it will be beneficial to put together,
in the brief form adopted in these pages, the results
deducible from recent discoveries. The free use of his
brother's materials will, it is conceived, give the work a
value, even with the most erudite; but its principal aim
is, to place, in a cheap and commodious form before the
popular reader, the means of gratifying curiosity upon a
subject often referred to, and of the existence of which, as
a successful result of modern research, few are entirely
ignorant.

If the following pages shall have the effect of com-
municating information to readers, who have hitherto
been deterred by the learning, or by the cost of the

more elaborate works which have appeared, and so
should stimulate curiosity, and excite a wider interest in
respect to these discoveries, the Author's object will be
gained.   The present Note is confined to Bactro-Arian
relics, but the late Mr. James Prinsep's cabinet is richer
far in coins of India, Boodhist, and Brahminical, extending
from periods of the most remote antiquity to the date of
Mahomedan conquest; and for these a separate study,
and if the subject be of sufficient general interest, a
separate Note of explanation may be required.

LIST OF PLATES.

ERRATA.

HISTORICAL RESULTS, &c.

ARIA, ARIANA, BACTRIA. These are names that every one has met with in the course of his reading, but very few know the precise locality of the regions so called,* and fewer still their history. The ancient authors of Greece and Rome furnish only some stray notices of kings who have conquered and reigned in those countries ; but neither kings nor kingdoms are ever mentioned, except incidentally because of their coming in contact with nations of the West; and we seek in vain for any consistent account of the dynasties which rose and fell, or even of the races that came and went, conquering and conquered, during the thousand years that followed the conquest and settlement of

---

* Aria is the territory of which Herat is the Capital. Ariana (Eeran) is the general name for the country east of Persia and Media, as far as the Indus. Bactria is the country watered by the Oxus and its tributaries. Soghdiana the mountains which feed the Jaxartes, and divide the two rivers.

B

these regions by Alexander of Macedon, the son of Philip.

We know, indeed, that for two hundred years after that epoch the kings of Bactria, and of Ariana, or Afghânistan, were Greek in name and by race, and that the language of their coins and official documents was Greek; still such was the indifference, or such the difficulty of communication, that little or no intercourse was maintained by the people of the West with these Eastern colonies; and though using a common language, and derived from the same stock with the nation which boasted at the period its pre-eminence in intelligence and civilization, they are never referred to except as a *terra incognita*, that few knew and none cared about.

The whole of Western and Central Asia was, it is true, the scene of continuous strife and convulsion during the entire period of Greek ascendancy in these regions, and the events of most prominent interest in the world were occurring at the time in the West, which may account for some indifference towards the petty struggles for power amongst isolated chiefs and colonies in the far East. But the information left us of the acts and expeditions of western kings in this quarter, and even of Alexander himself, is exceedingly scanty and imperfect, and we seek in vain for any reason why it should be so. The reading public of the nineteenth century, who wade through volumes of controversy upon single events of local history,

and who study accuracy, and the minutiæ of great
men's proceedings and motives, with a mawkish and
tedious interest, may well wonder to find so little
curiosity displayed by the ancients, not only as to
what was passing in Aria and Bactria, but even
regarding the expeditions of Alexander, Seleucus,
and Antiochus ; and it is the more surprising that
we have no consistent account in detail of the
actions and enterprises of these kings, and especially
of the first of them who so widely extended Greek
dominion and Greek civilization, when such an
example of correct and reasoning history had been
set by Thucydides, and when we know the pains
taken by Alexander himself to cultivate the opinion
of the learned of Greece, and to promote and encourage literature for the advancement of his own fame.

If, however, any man has a right to complain of
the treatment he receives from history, and to
lament the want of the *vatis sacri* to represent his
actions and character in a true light to posterity,
it is Alexander. The only justice done to him
is in the affix of the title Great, which his name
will carry with it to all time : we have little else
regarding him but shallow superficial gossip, and
libellous anecdotes, circulated with a view to detrac-
tion by the party which his genius and ascendancy
excluded from power. It is from such materials
that mankind is left to form its judgment upon the
man, who holds amongst Greeks even a higher place
than Julius Cæsar amongst Romans, and whose
fame even Cæsar envied.

We do not refer here to the mere school impressions formed from Plutarch and others, of Alexander's rashness and violence, of his passion and drunkenness, his ambition for false glory, and his vain desire for deification, but to the means we possess of following this conqueror in the great enterprises he successfully carried through, and of marking the changes he effected or contemplated in the institutions and social condition of the world. There is nothing like a philosophical history, or even a true account in detail of Alexander's exploits and proceedings, in all the literature of Greece and Rome, for assuredly the works of Arrian and Quintus Curtius do not deserve that character.

In tracing, therefore, the history of the colonies which Alexander planted in the East, the first difficulty experienced arises from the very imperfect notices handed down to us, of the means by which he established those colonies, of their number and position, of the arrangements made for their internal government, and, what is of even more importance, of their relations with the natives of the regions in which they were placed.

It is well remaiked by Professor Lassen, that Bactria and Aria, that is, the countries lying on either side of the Hindoo Koosh, between the Oxus and Indus rivers, are on the high road of Asiatic conquest, and have been the battle-field of every tribe and nation that has risen to dominion in the East. The history of this tract, therefore, if we had it com-

plete and continuous, would tell more of the history
of the world, and of the great revolutions in language, religion, civilization, and government, which
have been brought about by conquest, and by the
admixture of races resulting from conquest, than
that of any other country on the face of the earth.
For the want of this history, even for the period
when Greek dominion and the Greek language
gave means and facilities for preserving it, the
modern learned are driven to speculation and conjecture, groping their way in dark uncertainty, and
putting together facts gathered here and there at
wide intervals, or drawing inferences from vague
analogies of language, of feature, and of customs,
whereon they build theories, which are overturned
as fast as they are constructed.

It is now a little more than a century (1738)
since Bayer wrote his treatise in Latin on the
Greek colonies of Bactria, and proved to conviction,
as the same Professor observes, the neglect these
regions had experienced from writers of antiquity,
by the meagreness of the details his industry and
learning could discover in their works. He gave
the names of not more than six kings of Greek
origin, whom he found incidentally mentioned as
having reigned in these countries, but the dates of
their accessions and deaths, even the localities of
the dominion of several, were left, and still remain,
in uncertainty. It is only through coins since discovered, or by means of relics and inscriptions
obtained in topes or tumuli, that we have made, or

can hope to make, any advance in the knowledge of
the past history of these regions beyond the point
reached by Bayer, and the advance yet made is confined to a lengthened list of names, derived from
coins, of kings before unheard of and unknown; but
the coins, either by their execution, or by their type
and emblems, or by the titles and superscriptions,
afford circumstances from which to draw conclu-
sions as to the connection of the kings with one
another, or with known dynasties of the West.
Moreover, the number and localities in which the
coins are found, are circumstances from which to
deduce arguments, as to the length of reigns and
seats of government.   Next to inscriptions, therefore, coins are the best evidence we can obtain, to
support or supply the want of history.   We have
a few inscriptions, likewise, but they are in the
new Arian language, and the decyphering of them
remains to be accomplished.

It is not our purpose here to give in detail the
history of the discoveries made in Bactrian numis-
matics.   This has been well done by Professor
Wilson in the publication prepared by him, and
issued under the authority of the East India Company, for the purpose of giving to the world the
results of Mr. Masson's researches, a work that
does infinite honour to the patronage of that liberal
and enlightened body.   We will merely mention,
that, until within the last ten years, the progress
made in discovery was confined to occasional notices
of stray coins with Greek names, which found

their way to the cabinets of Europe, and were, by
the learned, presumed to be Bactrian, because the
coins were traced to that region, or to its vicinity,
and were not ascribable to other known dynasties.
But since the mission to Kâbool and Bokhâra of
the late Sir Alexander Burnes in 1831-32, there
has been thrown quite a new light upon this branch
of archæology, through the researches and discoveries of that officer, and of those engaged with
him in that and subsequent missions, and especially through the impulse and direction given to
the enquiries of others, who had even better oppor-
tunities than Burnes himself for prosecuting them.
We refer in particular to the European officers in the
service of Runjeet Singh, the ruler of the Punjab
and Peshawur, amongst whom Generals Ventura,
Alard and Court, are pre-eminent for the zeal with
which they have applied themselves to such investigations.   The great tope of Manykyâla was
opened by General Ventura in April and May,
1830, when some coins and very curious relics
were obtained.   The example was followed some
years after by General Court, who opened several
other topes in the same vicinity.   All these officers
obtained rich rewards for their labours, and taking
prompt means to make the results public, contributed greatly to advance the progress of discovery.
But Dr. Hœnigberger, of the same service, was the
first to draw the attention of Europe to the richness
of the field for antiquities presented by Afghânistan;

for, returning in 1834 through Kâbool, Bulkh, Bokhâra, and Orenburgh, he brought with him a large
collection of coins and relics made along that
route, as well as in the Punjâb, and exhibited
them in Germany, and afterwards in Paris, where
they excited much curiosity, and were the subject of
much learned speculation.

Nevertheless, it is to Mr. Masson, a private
adventurer, who long resided at Kâbool, and enjoyed
there the intimacy of the Nuwâb Jubâr Khan, and
the powerful protection of his brother, Ameer Dost
Mohummed, that we are indebted for the most
complete and best directed local researches that
have yet been made in these regions. Under the
countenance, and with the aid of these brothers,
Mr. Masson was able to employ himself for several
years in seeking remains of the Greek dynasties,
which had reigned in ancient times in the valley of
the Kâbool river. He visited the supposed sites of
various cities there, and identified the ruins, as
well as the localities, as fit capitals for these extinct
kingdoms; he opened likewise a great number of
topes, or tumuli, at Daranta, near Julâlabad, and
elsewhere in the same region, extracting from
them relics of all kinds ; and, thus having me-
ployed six or eight years in collecting antiquities
of the period of Greek and Scythian rule, (the
coins he procured at Beghrâm, the presumed site
of Alexandria *apud Caucasum*, are numbered by
tens of thousands), he transmitted the whole to the

Museum of the India House, where they are now deposited, and lie open to the ready inspection of the curious and learned.

These investigations, be it observed, were prosecuted, and the results made known, some time before the British army advanced to Kâbool. We are indebted to that expedition for a great advance in our knowledge of the geography of the region of discovery; but in other departments of science, especially in numismatic and archæological researches, little further fruit was obtained. The harvest had already been gathered in, and the busy occupations of war and diplomacy afforded little leisure for the closer search required to glean the scattered remnant, and to pick up what had escaped those who had taken the lead in this field.

There may, however, be another reason, besides want of leisure, for the sudden arrestation of the progress of discovery, just at the period of British occupation of the country, in which it had made such rapid strides. In 1838, while the army was on its march to Afghânistan, the individual in India, who had done most to instigate enquiry, and to make public the results obtained, who brought to bear on each discovery a power of ingenious reasoning, acute comparison, and deep study, that made it tell as a step in advance, rewarding those who had contributed to bring it to light, and attracting new interest to the pursuit, was suddenly withdrawn from these favorite studies by an illness, which terminated in death. The journal of the Asiatic Society, established and conducted by Mr. James Prinsep at Calcutta, ceased after the year mentioned to be the inspiring organ to encourage and direct researches in this particular field. There wanted, when he was gone, the Promethean spark to kindle into light and life the dust and ashes dug out of these interesting ruins, and to extract language and sense from the rude characters, found traced on the venerable remains and relics obtained from them.

In the same year (1838) Europe lost Mons. Jacquet, a promising scholar of Paris, who, in the same field of Eastern archæological research, rivalled, and sometimes anticipated, the discoveries of James Prinsep in India. All, however, who have signalized themselves by successful study in this department are not gone. There is yet much to hope from the labours of Professors Lassen and Wilson, and we do not despair of finding some one of those who enjoyed the friendship and shared the studies of James Prinsep, who may yield to the desire of prosecuting these researches with Indian aids, and who may, perhaps, turn to equally good account the many facilities and advantages, there available.*

At present, having before us the various papers which appeared in the journal of the Asiatic Society, with Professor Wilson's exhibition of the results of

---

* We have reason to believe that Lieut. Cunningham, of the Bengal Engineers, is preparing a work on the antiquities of India and Afghanistan.

Mr. Masson's discoveries and researches; having, also, Professor Lassen's work on Bactrian and Indo-Scythian History, which was translated and published in the Indian journal, we take these as helping us to reach a landing place in this branch of discovery, beyond which it will require time, and a new series of efforts and researches to make further progress; and so regarding them, we shall endeavour to give such a summary of the results established as will make the general reader familiar with a subject, reserved hitherto for the learned antiquarian.

Professor Wilson has, in his publication of Mr. Masson's researches,* devoted a chapter to the collection of notices regarding Aria and Ariana from ancient writers, and in this work of labour and research he has effected all that the scholar can desire, and more than those, to whom we address ourselves, can need for preparation. He has, also, rightly judged, that for the proper comprehension of the subject it is indispensable to follow Alexander in his marches and encampments in these regions. We cannot, however, understand why, having carried Alexander through the country south of the Imaus, or Hindoo Koosh, to his cantonment of Alexandria at Beghrâm, near Kâbool, the Professor should

* Ariana Antiqua—a Descriptive Account of the Antiquities and Coins of Afghanistan, with a Memoir on the Buildings called Topes, by C. Masson, Esq., by H. H. Wilson, Esq., M.A., F.R.S. London, 1841.

altogether omit in this part of his work* the operations of two entire seasons in Bactria, north of that
range, and proceed with Alexander's march to the
Indus, as if these two campaigns had not intervened;
for, in fact, it was in Bactria that the Greek power
was most firmly established, and the march to the
Punjâb would have been unsafe, if not imprac-
ticable, if that country had not been first reduced
and colonized, so as to prevent Bessus and the
Scythians from breaking in upon the line of communication with Media and Greece.

We shall also now briefly trace the march of
Alexander, including these northern campaigns.
The territory acquired by them, lying between
the Hindoo Koosh and the Sir or Jaxartes, was
much the richer and more important possession.
It contained, according to Justin, a thousand popu-
lous cities, and was held by an army in the field
of 15,000 men.   Such was the force left by Alexander under Amyntas, to cover and support his
colonies in Bactria, when he moved against India,
and the condition of the tribes on the northern
frontier required evidently the perpetual demon-
stration of readiness to repel and punish aggression,
which only such an army could provide.   When

* Professor Wilson does, in a different part of his work,
viz., when treating of the geography of ancient Bactria, state
the line of Alexander's march to the Jaxartes, but very briefly,
and the continuity of the narrative of the expedition is lost by
this division of the subject.

Bactria ultimately revolted from the Syrian kings, Aria and Afghânistan, or Ariana, followed with it, and the history of the one is so mixed up with the other, that the allotment of kings to either division at the time of separation, and the determination of the epochs of general sovereignty over both, are the main work by which the skill of the critic and antiquarian has to be tested.   But it is not Bactria only that is closely linked with Ariana : we do not see how Parthia, and the rise and fall of Arsacidan power therein, can well be excluded from an enquiry into the history of these regions.   For not only was the establishment of that dynasty contemporaneous with the revolt of Ariana and Bactria, and the relations between the three countries always inti-mate, but many of the Parthian kings extended their dominion over all three, and we find Par-thian kings, and kings of kings, amongst those whose coins and relics are the materials, upon which we have to build the new fabric of history which is the result of recent discoveries.

To begin with the original conquest and coloni-zation of these countries by the Greeks, Arrian tells us that Alexander the Great, after the pursuit and death of Darius, returned to the Caspian Sea, to complete the conquest of Hyrcania and of the Mardi.   This was in June and July 330 B.C. The colonies here planted were the nucleus and main strength of the Parthian sovereignty, esta-blished eighty years afterwards by Arsaces.   In August or September of the same year,   Alexander

marched into Aria and established a garrison, with
a Persian Satrap, at Susia, its then capital. Professor Wilson finds on the map a place called
Zuzan, on the desert side of the mountains west of
Herât, and supposes that to be the Susia mentioned
by Arrian. Dr. Thirlwall in his history identifies
Susia with Toos, which is far within the Parthian frontier. We incline to the opinion that
Subzâr or Subza-wâr, a city south of Herât, and
within the region of fertility, is the Susia referred
to, and certainly it is by situation a much more
likely place for the capital indicated, than either of
the other two. The garrison left here was overpowered as soon as Alexander had crossed the
mountains in pursuit of Bessus, whereupon, returning hastily, he re-took the city, and capturing
Artachaona* also, a place of refuge in the hills to the
east of Susia, continued his operations southward to
the Pontus, or Inland Sea, in which the Helmund
terminates. Subzâr is in the direct line of such
a march, which is another reason for preferring it for
the capital of Aria. Alexander now effectually
subjugated the entire country south of the Paropamisus, and placed Governors in Seestan and
Arachotia, that is at Kandahar, or in Arghundab,
which Professor Wilson, with good reason, considers

---

* Mr. Elphinstone considers Artachaona to be Herât, but
that could scarcely have been the stronghold of refuge, to
which the revolting Persian would retire, being on the direct
line of march to Bactria from Seestan. Sakhir, the capital
of the Ghoris, is a much more likely position.

to be that region. He also placed a colony in a new city, built to control the Arians, which all authorities concur in regarding as the foundation of the afterwards, and still famous city of Herât. From this point, starting in the end of October, Alexander marched to the Kâbool valley, through a country occupied by Indians, and bordering on Arachotia, and his troops suffered exceedingly in the march from want, snow, and cold. We think the line of this march was the upper or hill route from Herât, running close under, and amongst the hills of the Paropamisan range, a region then occupied, according to all authorities, by an Indian race; and in confirmation of this line of march, we have the fact given by Arrian, that immediately on Alexander's return across the Hindoo Koosh from Bactria, his first act was to change the governor he had left in the Paropamisus, which shows that he had previously marched through and subjugated that hill country. Besides, the time (October) was short for a circuitous march, and if he had taken the route by Kandahar, and found snow in that vicinity, the passage by Ghuznee would have been quite closed, as we know by the sad experience of disasters in consequence.

The cantonment in which Alexander's army passed the winter of 330-29 B.C. was the Alexandria *apud Caucasum*,* the site of which has been

---

* Professor Wilson is inclined to the opinion that the ancient city, of which ruins are found at Beghrâm, was Nicæa, and that Alexandria was closer under the mountains in the Ghorbund

traced on the plain of Beghram near Chârikar, about thirty or forty miles north of Kabool. It is here that coins of the Greco-Bactrian kings and of their Scythian successors, have been found in much greater profusion than any where else, the place is likely, therefore, to have been the Capital of the region of the Kophen or Kâbool river.

Early in 329 B. C. Alexander crossed the Hindoo Koosh, and captured Drapsacus, or Indrâb. Thence, marching down the Oxus, he occupied and established garrisons in the country between that river and the mountains, while Bessus flying northward, across the Oxus, to Nautaka, or Karshi, was pursued and captured there by Ptolemy. Alexander then marched to Markanda, or Samarcand, and drove the Scythians before him to the Sir or Jaxartes, which river he crossed, and gained a great battle on the mountains opposite to Khojund. On the Jaxartes Alexander remained some time, establishing colonies for the defence of the passage of that river against Scythian incursion. While he was so occupied, Spitamenes came from the Kuzil Koom Desert and fell on Markanda in his rear. Though this partizan leader failed to capture the town of Markanda, he overpowered and cut to

valley. Beghrâm, however, is the more important position, commanding all the passes to Koondooz, and Khoolum east of the Kohi-Baba mountain, and seems much better adapted for a cantonment, and capital city, than a site in the close valley higher up. It appears, therefore, more likely to be the Alexandria referred to, which was the larger and more famous city of the two.

pieces a division of the Grecian army sent for its
reinforcement; whereupon, Alexander counter-
marching, took Kuropolis, which we suppose to be
the ancient Kêsh, now Shuhur-Subz, and ravaged
the entire valley of the Zurafshâr, the Polytime-
tus, or Samarkand river. As the year 329 B. c.
was drawing to a close, when these operations were
concluded, Alexander wintered his army at Ariaspe,
or Zariâspe, which for many reasons we conclude
to be Hazârasp ; First, because of its being in a
military point of view the best position he could
occupy in advance to check Spitamenes, being on
the border of the desert, with the Oxus available
to bring down his supplies.   Secondly, because
it is on the borders of Kharizm, and he was here
in close communication with the Khorasmeni.
Thirdly, because, while in this cantonment, he
received a mission from the banks of the Wolga,
for intercourse with which region it lies convenient,
and lastly, from the great similarity of the name.

In the spring of 328 B. c., Alexander took the
field in five divisions, to reduce the entire country
between the Oxus and Jaxartes.   Spitamenes was
defeated, and slain at the beginning of the campaign, after a vain attempt to surprise Ariaspe,
which confirms its identity with Hazârasp, a place
well in advance, and, therefore, subject to such
an attack.   The rest of the season was devoted to
the reduction of the numerous strongholds in the
upper part of Soghdiana, and Mâwur-oon-nuhur,
and to the establishment of colonies and garrisons

to hold the country subdued. The winter of 328
—27, B. C. was passed at Nautaka, or Karshi, and
in the spring of 327, B. C. Alexander recrossed the
Hindoo Koosh, and from Alexandria *apud Caucasum* commenced operations to reduce the country
between that range and the Sofed-koh, that is in
the Kohistân and Kâbool valley to the Indus.
Alexander himself commanded to the north of the
Kophen, or Kâbool river, and Hephœstion with
Taxiles, the Indian king, took the route to the
south. The latter arriving first at Attuk, built
there the bridge of boats, by which Alexander's
army passed into the Punjâb. Professors Lassen
and Wilson follow these operations in considerable
detail, adopting Arrian's report of them, which is
confirmed by what we now know of the geography
of the entire tract. For our present purpose, it is
sufficient to state briefly that this entire country
was subdued, and colonized like Bactria, in the
months of April and May, 327 B. C. In July,
327 B. C. Porus was defeated on its banks of the
Jihlum, and the months following were spent in
colonizing and reducing the Punjâb, and in building a fleet for the descent of the Indus.

The greater part of 326 B. C. was passed in the
passage down that river, and in operations to reduce the different races which occupied its banks.
At the close of the rainy season, that is in about
September or October, 326 B. C. Alexander commenced his return march in three divisions. The
first, with the heavy baggage, he sent by Kandahar

and Seestân, under Craterus. The second he led
himself, by the sea coast, through Baloochistân
and Makrân to Karmania (Kărmân). A third he
sent by the then unexplored sea-route to the Persian
Gulf, under Nearchus. All met at Suza towards
the close of 325 B. C., the greatest hardships having
been encountered by Alexander himself, in passing
the arid deserts of southern Persia.

The result of these operations was, not merely
that the conquering army swept over the face of
Asia, leaving, like Tymoor, Chungeez Khan, and
Attila, marks of ravage and desolation only in the
regions traversed, but that the whole of the wide
tract of country from the Mediterranean to the
Indus, and from the Jaxartes and Caspian to the
Sea, was subdued, garrisoned, and colonised,—
made, in short, part of the Grecian empire, thus
completely established in the East. We do not
hear that any where the native population rebelled,
and threw off the Grecian yoke, or overpowered
the garrisons left to maintain possession of the
country, excepting only in the Punjâb, near
twenty years afterwards, during the troubles which
followed the decease of Alexander. Everywhere
else, the government and the armies were Greek ;
Hellenism was the system upon which the adminis-
tration was organised and conducted, and society
and religion yielded to the ascendancy of this domi-
nant principle.

Alexander died in the spring of 323 B. C., that
is, in the second year after his return to the ancient

capitals of the Persian and Assyrian kings, leaving
only a posthumous son.   He caught a fever in the
marshes of Mesopotamia, while planning a fresh
capital for this vast empire in that central region.
Consequently, we can only conjecture, what might
have been the result, if his life had been spared to
the ordinary average of human existence, or if an
able successor had been left, to perfect the arrangements he had so auspiciously commenced, and to
consolidate, secure, and completely Hellenise this
wide dominion.   But Alexander's empire, though
of only ten years growth, was by no means tran-
sient.   His colonies, and their institutions, manners,
and language had struck deep root even in this
short period, and we shall find that the impulse
towards Hellenism had a lasting action in central
Asia, the effects of which were felt for at least five
hundred years after the decease of the conqueror.
It is the especial object of these pages to endeavour
to trace out this action in the regions where it had
to maintain a struggle with barbarism, and to show
how it finally sunk, and was extinguished, without
exciting even a passing regret, or receiving the
notice of a recording sentence, from any historian or
writer of the distant West.

Alexander left, as above stated, no successor, for
his brother Aridæus, and the posthumous child of
Roshuna, or Roxana, called Alexander after his
father, can scarcely be so considered.   The consequence was, that the marshals, and men in power,
became each independent, refusing obedience to

their equals, or to any council of such at head-quarters.

The only system of government Alexander had had time to organize, was that of military occu-pation, and, of course, the military commandant of each district was the satrap, in whose person, and through whom, every authority of the state was locally exercised. While Alexander lived, the power of removal being absolute, and arbitrarily exerted, these satraps were effectually held in check; for none dared refuse a summons to the pre-sence to answer a complaint, or to render account of any doubtful action; but on his death, the annihi-lation of this controling power, which existed but in the prestige of the conqueror's name and character, was immediate. There was no method of control-ing, removing, or punishing a military satrap, but to direct against him the arms of a rival neighbour. In this manner Eumenes, the Governor of Cappa-docia (B. C. 322), was employed against Craterus, whom he defeated and slew in action; and, being proscribed for this success by the Macedonians who loved Craterus, Antigonus (B. C. 320), was similarly employed against him. Eumenes was now worsted in turn, and driven out of Asia Minor (B. C. 318, 317); but jealousy of Antigonus led to his being re-employed against that chief, and the war between them was carried into Media and Parthia. Eumenes maintained the struggle for two years with eminent skill and good success, notwithstanding the ill-will of the Macedonians.

In the third campaign (B.C. 315), however, after a
victory gained, he was delivered up prisoner to his
rival by his own troops, and Antigonus becoming
in consequence the sovereign of Asia, assumed
openly the regal title.   His first act after the overthrow of his rival was, to send the Argyraspides,
Silvershields, a favored corps of *emeriti,* to be worn
out by the hard duty of Arachotia, as a punishment
for their bad faith to Eumenes. Seleucus (B. C. 314),
Governor of Babylon, was soon after dispossessed
by Antigonus, and fled to Ptolemy, whom he
instigated to oppose Antigonus.   The two invaded
Syria and Phœnicia from Egypt (B.C. 312), and
gaining some advantage, Seleucus started thence
with 1000 men, and recovered Babylon, the population of which was friendly to him.   Thence,
influencing the garrisons of Media and Persia, he
expelled the Governors for Antigonus, who was so
occupied by his war with Ptolemy, that he could
only send lieutenants against Seleucus, and these
were successively defeated.   In 305 B.C., Seleucus
gaining a great victory over Nicanor, one of these
lieutenants, followed it up by seizing and adding to
his own government, the whole of Media, Hyrcania,
Parthia, Bactria, and Aria, and all the countries as
far as the Indus.   In 303, he crossed that river
to make war on Chundra Goopta (Sandracottus),
who, during these contentions, had expelled the
Grecian garrisons from the Punjâb, and had so
recovered that country for the native sovereigns of
India. Seleucus made, however, a hasty peace

with Chundra Goopta, ceding the Punjâb as far as
the Indus,* and receiving 500 elephants, being called
back suddenly for a final struggle with Antigonus.
In this war with that chief, Lysimachus assisted
from Thrace, as well as Ptolemy from Egypt, and
Antigonus being driven into Phrygia, was there
defeated and slain by Seleucus in 301 B.C.
From this period till 280 B.C., when Seleucus
Nicator was assassinated by Ptolemy Ceraunus,
after a victory gained over Lysimachus, in which
that king also was slain, the whole of Asia to the
Indus and Jaxartes, was under the Syrian king.
The son of Seleucus, Antiochus Soter, from 280 to
261 B.C., reigned also undisturbed over the same
territory, and left it to his son, Antiochus Theus.
This last king, however, getting involved in a difficult
war with Ptolemy Philadelphus, and his successor,
Euergetes, neglected his Eastern possessions. Bactria, in consequence, declared its independence
under Theodotus, or Diodotus, in 256, or 255 B.C.
according to Bayer. Parthia followed about the year†
250 B.C., the revolt of this province being ascribed
to an attempt of Agathocles, the local Governor,
upon the person of a noble youth named Tiridates,
which his brother, Arsaces, resented by conspiring

* Strabo says Arachotia was also ceded, but this seems
doubtful. Kuchchee to the Bolan Pass, with the Valley of
the Indus, may be the region intended.

† Vaillant gives the year 256 B.C. for the date of Arsaces'
revolt in Parthia, basing the date on the consuls, named by
Justin as in office for the year. The year 250 B.C. seems,
however, preferably established.

and slaying the Governor. To secure himself, he seized the government, and the revolt being neglected, he continued to strengthen himself, until in 241 B.C., he was able to add Hyrcania to his original government of Parthia, which lay between Herât and the Caspian, and is now the province of which Mushud is the capital.*

The native country of Arsaces is uncertain. By some he is called a Dahian, that is, a native of Soghd. By others, a Bactrian. Moses of Chorene, the historian of Armenia, who lived in the fifth century of our era, when the Arsacidan dynasties had recently been expelled from both Parthia and Armenia, declares the first Arsaces to have been a native of Bulkh. He adds, that the dynasty were called Balhavenses, or Pahlaveean, from the circumstance that Bulkh was added to Parthia, and made its seat of Government, by the son of Arsaces, meaning Mithridates, the great-grandson. Strabo says that Arsaces was a Bactrian, who had fled to Parthia, because the rival party of Theodotus had prevailed in his native city, which is not at all inconsistent with the Armenian's story. We give in a note below the words of Moses from the Latin translation,† because the passages are curious, and contain the earliest mention we find anywhere of

* The Persians consider Khorasan to include Herât and the Paropamisus, and northward to extend as far as Merv, otherwise Parthia might be described by that name.

† Itaque, ut diximus, post sexaginta annos, quam Alexander mortuus est, Parthis imperitavit Arsaces, fortis in urbe orientis quæ vocatur *Balcha* in regione Cusæorum. (Qy. Hindoo

the city of Bulkh, by that name, showing that it
could not well be identical with Ariaspe, as is by
some supposed.

Whatever may have been the country and race
to which Arsaces belonged, we find him using
Greek only on his coins, and in his public letters
and correspondence. There is no other language
or character found on any coin of known Parthian mintage and type. Some coins indeed, with
Parthian names and bilingual superscriptions, and
one of an Arsaces, have recently been discovered
in Afghanistân, and on them we find the Parthian
title of king of kings : still, it is doubtful whether
these are the coins of Parthian kings of kings, or
of Satraps, who declared their independence, and
assumed that lofty title; and, even if some of them
be coins of real sovereigns of Parthia, they will
have been minted locally, to provide a local
currency for Afghanistân.

The Arsacidan coins of Parthia proper, have
ordinarily the sovereign's head, without any in-

Koosh) posita.—Book II., cap. II. p. 54.—again in page 188,
De regiis stupibus. " Tum filius ejus, Arsaces, qui cognomi-
natus est magnus, qui Antiochum occidit, Volarsacem fratrem
suum Armeniæ regem fecit, et ab se secundum constituit. Ipse
autem, *Balham* profectus, regnum suum ibi fundavit: ac
propterea progenies ejus Balhavenses nominatur, sicut Volar-
sacis fratris sui proles, ab progenitore, Arsacidum nomen
invenit; illi autem sunt reges Balhavenses.

N.B. The Arsaces here referred to, who set up his brother
in Armenia, and established his own sovereignty in Bulkh was
Mithridates Ist.

scription on one side ; on the other, a sitting
figure with a bow held out, and the inscription in
Greek on four sides, forming a square on the face
of the coin.* This inscription has seldom any but
the family name of Arsaces, with the title ΒΑΣΙΛΕΥΣ
or ΒΑΣΙΛΕΥΣ ΒΑΣΙΛΕΩΝ, and various epithets,
ΜΕΓΑΣ, ΔΙΚΑΙΟΣ, ΕΠΙΦΑΝΗΣ, ΕΥΕΡΓΕΤΗΣ,
ΖΗΝΙΟΣ, or ΞΕΙΝΙΟΣ, ΘΕΟΣ, ΝΙΚΑΤΩΡ, ΦΙΛΕΛΛΗ-
ΝΟΣ, ΘΕΟΠΑΤΗΡ, &c. all pure Greek, and generally
in the genitive case. Only one of the Bilingual
coins of Afghanistan yet found, has the family
name of Arsaces on it, and all these coins, as we
shall show hereafter, differ in other respects from
those of known Arsacidan type. It is not easy
to classify, and assign the Arsacidan coins to the
known sovereigns of Parthia, for the name Arsaces
is, as above stated, common to all, and history
does not tell us which of the race took the particular
epithets and titles we find on them. But we have
this criterion, that Basileus only, or with such
epithets as just, illustrious, and other modest titles
of that kind, will indicate the earliest of the race.
Great king of kings was the title first assumed

* Some of Vonones have his name on the obverse, in imitation probably of the Romans, amongst whom he was educated :
one of these is given by Professor Wilson, for comparison with
the Afghan coins of the same name. It has on the reverse a
Victory, instead of the sitting figure with a bow : and several
of the later Arsacidan kings coined also with a winged
Victory presenting a crown, on the reverse, which is a device
we find on the Ario-Parthian coins. The obverse, however,
of these latter is widely different.

by Mithridates II., which Asiatic form must have
been adopted after the conquest and acquisition of
countries bordering on India, for we find the
same title on coins of Scythian kings, who acquired
dominion in those regions at the same period, and
we have reason to believe it to be of Indian origin.
There is at the India House a very complete
cabinet of Arsacidan coins, which was presented to
the East India Company by Sir H. Willock, now
deputy chairman. We doubt if any other Museum
has one so full. It will be seen upon examination
of the coins, that the earliest have on the obverse
the helmeted head of a young man with no inscription at all ; on the reverse, is the sitting figure above
described, with a bow, and the simple legend,
ΑΡΣΑΚΟΥ ΒΑΣΙΛΕΩΣ. This coin we cannot hesi-
tate to assign to the first Arsaces. Next, we have
the same helmeted head, with an inscription on the
reverse, bearing the same sitting figure, ΑΡΣΑΚΟΥ
ΒΑΣΙΛΕΩΣ ΜΕΓΑΛΟΥ, which may be of the same
king, after his defeat and capture of Seleucus, an
exploit entitling him to the epithet. Then we have
the same inscription, and reverse, with a filleted head
on the obverse, having the hair full over the shoulders,
as is usual with kings of this race. Next, we have a
similar filleted head, with a similar reverse, and the
inscription ΑΡΣΑΚΟΥ ΒΑΣΙΛΕΩΣ ΕΠΙΦΑΝΟΥΣ.
A fifth variety has, with a nearly similar obverse and
reverse, the inscription ΑΡΣΑΚΟΥ ΦΙΛΟΠΑΤΡΟΣ
ΒΑΣΙΛΕΩΣ ΜΕΓΑΛΟΥ, which word, Philopater is
considered by numismatists to denote association

with the father while living; but history is silent
as to which of the early Arsacides falls within this
category. A sixth variety has, on a similar coin in
other respects, the inscription, ΑΡΣΑΚΟΥ ΘΕΟ-
ΠΡΟΠΟΥ ΒΑΣΙΛΕΩΣ ΜΕΓΑΛΟΥ. If we assign
these six varieties to the predecessors of Mithridates II.*, he will be the first crowned king of kings
of this race; and, as his reign was one of Arsacidan
greatest power and pride, the evidence of coins
supports and confirms that of history. The early
coins we have noticed are not mentioned by Vaillant,
but Mionnet in his great work has supplied the
omission, and corrected Vaillant's very arbitrary
and capricious allotment of coins to kings of this race;
Visconti and several other foreign numismatists have
also devoted themselves to this subject, so that
there is little new or original to be added at this
day. Nevertheless, Professor Wilson would have
made his work on Arianian relics more complete,
by including the series of Arsacidan coins contained in the cabinet referred to. Perhaps, however,
the description of them, as of the Sassanian series
in the same Museum, is reserved for the special
catalogue of the library and curiosities, which is
now under preparation.

We cannot take leave of this cabinet without

* Mithridates I. is by some supposed to have called himself
King of Kings; but the date of the reign of the second of the
name is more consistent with the period when this title was
assumed in Bactria. Eucratides, the cotemporary of Mithridates I., only called himself Great King.

noticing especially two coins it contains of Arsacidan kings, which are historical, and very peculiar.
One bears the usual filleted head, with full locks,
and no inscription on the obverse; but on the
reverse has a female bust, with prominent Roman
features, and the superscription ΘΕΡΜΟΥΣΑΣ,
ΒΑΣΙΛΙΣΣΑΣ ΘΕΑΣ ΟΥΡΑΝΙΑΣ. This, of course,
is a coin of Phrahates, who married Thermusa, the
maid (Ancilla) presented to him by Anthony, and
who yielded to this queen's influence so far, as to
send his four other sons as hostages to Augustus,
in order to make way for the succession of her son,
Phrahataces, by whom he was soon after poisoned.
    The other peculiar coin is of Vonones, of which
there are three specimens. A drawing of it is
given by Professor Wilson in Plate XV. of his
Ariana, for comparison with the coins of Vonones,
found in Afghânistan. On one side is the head of
Vonones, with the simple inscription ΒΑΣΙΛΕΥΣ
ΟΝΩΝΗC in the nominative case, according to
Roman taste. On the reverse is a Victory, with
the inscription ΒΑΣΙΛΕΥC ΟΝΩΝΗC ΝΕΙΚΗCΑC
ΑΡΤΑΒΑΝΟΝ, thus identifying him as the son of
Phrahates, invited from Rome, and successful at
first against Artabanus, but expelled soon after.
The absence of any other coinage of this king con-
firms what Tacitus reports of his short lived power,
as the inscription does the manner of his accession.
    Having premised this, we will now shortly give
the dynasty of Arsacidan kings, with a notice of

such circumstances as are to be gathered from
Greek and Roman authors, in respect to each. We
have nowhere a consecutive history of the race or
country, written with authority from native records,
or at a period when events were recent, and the
succession of sovereigns easily traced and ascertained; but, of course, the notices of Parthia, in the
classic authors of Greece and Rome, are more frequent than those of Bactria, Aria, and countries
farther East, because Parthian kings came more frequently into collision with the sovereigns and
nations of Europe, and of Western Asia.

B.C. 254-250. ARSACES I., a native of Bulkh in
  Bactria, revolted from Antiochus Theus, slaying Agathocles, the Governor of Parthia. In
  241 B.C. he seized Hyrcania, and fearing invasion, prepared against a combined attack from
  Syria and Bactria; but Theodotus of Bactria
  dying, he entered into a strict alliance with
  the second Theodotus, and so awaited the
  attack from Syria. In 236 B.C. Seleucus Kal-
  linicus having made peace with Egypt, made
  a first expedition against Parthia, which was
  of little effect. In 230 B.C. he made a second
  expedition, in which he at first drove Arsaces
  into Khârizm, but was afterwards defeated and
  made prisoner by this king, who thereupon
  took the title of Megas Basileus. Arsaces is
  said to have been killed in action with Aria-
  rathes of Cappadocia, but the date and circum-

stances are not known.* Seleucus died by a
fall from his horse while returning from his
captivity.

About B.C. 220. II. ARSACES II. ARTABANUS,† son
of the last king, continued to extend and
strengthen the Parthian empire, adding Media
while Antiochus Magnus was at war with
Egypt. In 212, Antiochus commenced operations against Arsaces, and recovered Media.
Soon after, he drove Arsaces out of Parthia,
leaving him only Hyrcania. In 210, Antiochus
captured Syringis, a city of that country ; but
Arsaces calling in the Scythians, again made

* Vaillant quoting Arrian, *apud Syncellum*, supposes
Arsaces to have been killed in the second year after declaring
his independence, and to have been succeeded by his brother,
Tiridates. But we find nothing of this in Justin or Strabo, and
Arsaces' name would not have been carried down, if his life
and power had been so little enduring. The accession of
Tiridates, the brother, seems therefore very doubtful. Syncellus was a Byzantine, who lived in the time of Charlemagne.
He cites Arrian, in his Chronology, for the fact, that it was
Agathocles, and not Pherecles, who committed the outrage
which led to the insurrection ; and although it may thence be
inferred, that Arrian's Parthian History was then extant,
Syncellus does not take any other facts from it, nor refer to it
in support of his assignment of only two years for the reign of
the first Arsaces, in opposition to Justin and Strabo. It is
probable that one of the brothers died after two years, but not
Arsaces.

† Vaillant gives the year 217 B.C. for that of the accession of
Artabanus, allowing two years to the first Arsaces, and thirty-
seven to Tiridates, and following in this the Chronological
tables of Syncellus.

head with an army of 100,000 men, and in
208 B.C. Antiochus made peace with him, ceding
Parthia and Hyrcania in consideration of aid in
the war against Bactria and Aria. Polybius
calls the king opposed to Antiochus, Artabanus,
but other authorities describe him only as the
second Arsaces, son of the founder of the
dynasty. The date of his decease is not indicated with any certainty.

B.C. 196. III. ARSACES PRIAPATIUS, or PHRIADA-
TIUS, son of the last king. We know of no
occurrences of this reign, except that it lasted
fifteen years, was peaceable, and of good re-
pute, and that the king left three sons, all of
whom reigned; viz., Phrahates, Mithridates,
and Artabanes.

B.C. 181. IV. ARSACES PHRAHATES I. The Mardi
were reduced in this reign, but it was short
and inglorious.

B.C. 177. V. ARSACES MITHRIDATES I. The date
of accession is uncertain. Some placing it as
early as 180 B.C., and others as late as 165 B.C.
It is of this king that Moses of Chorene writes,
that he set up his brother in Armenia, and re-
moved the seat of his own government to
Bulkh, which he had subdued; all Media and
Persia, also, submitted to him at one time, and
he captured Babylon. In 140 B.C. Demetrius
Nicator attacked Parthia, and being joined by
many of the Greek colonists recently subjugated
by Mithridates, gained some successes, but in a

second campaign was made prisoner by treachery, according to Justin (*simulatione pacis*).
He was well treated, and married to a daughter
of the Parthian king, but did not recover his
liberty until released by Phrahates, when
Parthia was attacked again ten years after by
his brother. After the defeat of Demetrius,
Mithridates made a successful expedition into
India. He had previously brought under his
dominion the greater part of what had formed
the empire of his cotemporary, Eucratides;
that is, besides Western Bactria, Aria, Seestan,
and Arachotia; but Soghdiana was seized by
the Scythians.

B. C. 139. VI. ARSACES PHRAHATES II., son of
Mithridates, succeeded his father soon after
the expedition into India, but the exact date
is nowhere stated. In 131 B.C. Antiochus
Sidetes made war on Parthia with much success
at first, from the same cause that had favored
Demetrius; that is, the favor of the Greco-
Bactrians, who were disaffected towards Parthia; but in 130 B.C. he was defeated in a
great battle and slain. Phrahates had called
in the Scythians to aid in this war; after its
close, they committed ravages, to punish which,
Phrahates took the field against them, and was
slain in action. There is reason to believe
that Bactria was in this reign subjugated entirely by Scythians.

B.C. 126. VII. ARSACES ARTABANES, uncle of Phra-

hates, and youngest son of Priapatius, succeeded, but he too was wounded in an action
with the Tochari Scythians, and died of the
wound.

B.C. 115. VIII. ARSACES MITHRIDATES II., called
also *Great*, son of Artabanes, succeeded. He
gained advantages, and made some settlement
with the Scythians, and by their aid is supposed to have been established as nominal
sovereign over Western Bactria, Aria, and at
one time as far as the Indus in Southern
Afghanistan. The Scythians, however, are in
this reign supposed, under Azes and his successors, to have held dominion in Bulkh and
Kabool, and thence to have conquered the
Punjab. The Tochari, Yeutchi, or White
Huns, were settled under Asian kings in
Sogdiana, and the mountainous country north
of the Oxus. In the time of this king a letter
was addressed to Rome, and ambassadors came
from Mithridates to Sylla, the Dictator. He
died about 85 B.C. *gloriosâ senectute*, but the
date is uncertain.

B. C. 85. A period of contention and civil war
followed, and if the *kings of kings* of Parthian
race, whose coins are found in Afghanistan,
of pure Greek type, were a separate dynasty,
this will be the period when most probably
their independence was declared.

XI. MNASKIRES and X. PHRAHATES, are mentioned
as rivals for the throne of Parthia, but little

is known of either. The Scythians increased
in power during these troubles, and in 77 B.C.
placed a king on the Parthian throne.

B. C. 77. XI. ARSACES SINATRUX, or SANATROIKES,
as written on his coins. The Sakarauli
Scythians placed this king on the throne. A
letter to him from Mithridates of Pontus is
preserved in Sallust's fragments, but it can
scarcely be genuine, and seems to be of Roman
fabrication. His reign was marked by no
event of note.

B. C. 67. XII. ARSACES PHRAHATES III. son of Sinatrux, succeeded his father, and soon after
entered into treaty with Pompey, during the
war of Rome with Tigranes of Armenia. He
reigned peaceably for ten years. In 56 B. C.
his two sons, Orodes and Mithridates, conspired and slew him : then quarrelling for the
succession, Orodes prevailed, and Mithridates
sought refuge and succour from Gabinius,
Pompey's lieutenant, in Syria. But he being
called into Egypt, Mithridates attempted
alone to displace his brother, but was captured
and put to death.

B. C. 55. XIII. ARSACES ORODES reigned when
Crassus made his disastrous expedition, and
was defeated, and slain by Surenas. He also
was opposed to Ventidius, the lieutenant of
Anthony: and his favorite son and heir apparent
Pakores was defeated and slain by that general
in B. C. 39. Orodes much grieved at the loss,

nominated another son named Phrahates to
be his heir, and was by him circumvented
and slain.

B. C. 37. XIV. ARSACES PHRAHATES. A party
attempted to exclude this son for the parricide,
but with Scythian aid he established himself,
and was on the throne when Anthony invaded
Parthia, and penetrating 300 miles beyond
the Armenian frontier (the Kur river), laid
siege to Praaspa.* Failing in the siege, Anthony made a disastrous retreat. A brother
and rival of Phrahates, named Tiridates,
sought refuge and succour from Augustus
Cæsar after Anthony's death; and Augustus
using the opportunity, obtained from Phrahates restoration of the standards taken from
Crassus, with four sons of the king to reside
at Rome for education and as hostages. A fifth
son, Phrahataces, by the Italian queen, Thermusa, whose influence had sent away the hostages, conspired against his father, and got rid
of him by poison, in the year 4 A. D. but he
was not allowed to reign.

A. D. 4. XV. ARSACES ORODES II. Convulsions
followed the death of Phrahates, and Orodes,
a son, was set up, whose civil war with his

---

* Seleucia, on the Tigris, was the Capital in this reign, but
when it became so is uncertain. Anthony declared he would
treat when he arrived there, upon which the Parthian Ambas-
sador, said "Sooner will hair grow on the palms of these
hands than you take Seleucia."

parricide brother lasted nearly ten years.
Orodes was himself put to death for his
cruelty, about 14 A.D., and a son of Phrahates,
was asked from Rome.

A. D. 14. XVI. ARSACES VONONES the First,* was
sent by Tiberius Cæsar on the application of
a party at the capital of Parthia, and gaining
a victory over Artabanus, was established as
king in Seleucia. But becoming unpopular
from his un-Asiatic habits, Artabanus returned
and expelled him again, whereupon he retired
to Armenia, but being expelled thence also,
died in Syria.

A. D. 18. XVII. ARSACES ARTABANUS of Media,
said by Tacitus to be descended, on the mother's
side only, from Arsaces, and to have been
educated amongst the *Dahæ* Scythians, was
set up by them, and though unpopular for his
cruelty, maintained himself by the same means.
In A. D. 35, Tiberius sent from Rome a second
son of Phrahates, called by that name, and
Artabanus was expelled again from Seleucia,
and lived for a time in great extremity, in
the wilds of Hyrcania, but returned and again
drove out his rival. He died, leaving, accord-

* Vaillant in his Chronological Canon at the end of Vol. I.
says, Vonones was invited in A. D. 6, but in the annals at the
commencement, A. D. 14 is the date, and this seems preferable,
and more consistent with both Tacitus and Josephus. Professor Wilson has given a reign of twenty-four years to this
king, through the mistake of placing its commencement in
6 B. C., instead of 6 A. D., which latter date even is not warranted by authority.

ing to Josephus, seven sons, Darius, Bardanes, Gotarzes, Orodes, Volageses, Pakores, and Tiridates. Of these, according to the same author, he nominated Bardanes his successor, but according to Tacitus, he was slain by his brother Gotarzes, who seized and held the throne, until conquered by Bardanes.

A. D. 41. XVIII. ARSACES BARDANES. This king was in alliance with Rome. According to Josephus, his brothers yielded the sovereignty to him, but other authorities state that he overpowered them after a civil war.* His reign was glorious, though short. According to Tacitus, he extended his dominion as far as

* It is quite impossible to reconcile the account given by Josephus with the short but seemingly authoritative notice of these two kings, found in Tacitus; Josephus mentions them in connection with Izates of Adiabene, who embraced Judiasm, and was circumcised, and says that Artabanus, when expelled the second time from Seleucia, took refuge with Izates, and was by him restored : that dying soon after, he left the throne to Bardanes, whose name he writes Ουαρδανης, and that this king sought a confederacy with Izates against Rome, which he disapproving, was threatened in consequence with invasion. But the Parthians not disposed to a war with Rome, made away with Bardanes, and set up his brother Gotarzes, who also dying soon after, Vologeses, another brother, succeeded, and he assigned Media to his brother Pakores, and Armenia to another brother, Tiridates. All this is irreconcileable with the reported glories of Bardanes, in whose court Philostratus places Apollonius Tyaneus as a guest for some years, and makes him journey with his safeguard through Bactria to India ; and as this account of the impostor was written in the reign of Severus, it shows the received notions of the day respecting Bardanes.

the river Sinde ? the boundary of the country
of the Dahæ, which we conclude to be to the
Indus south, and north east as far as Sogh-
diana, then in the possession of the Yeutchi
Scythians, who had overpowered the Dahæ.
He was cut off by treachery while hunting.

A. D. 47. XIX. ARSACES GOTARZES (Persian Go-
durz), the next brother then succeeded. He
is declared by Tacitus to have been a worship-
per of Hercules, supported by Scythian auxi-
liaries. Claudius, the emperor, gave his countenance and active support to Mihardates, a
son of Vonones, the hostage king, but he
failed in an attempt on the throne of Parthia,
and Gotarzes died shortly after a natural
death.

A.D. 49. XX. ARSACES VONONES II. This reign
also was short and inglorious. The coins
ONΩNOΥ, found in Afghanistan, with the
title of king of kings in the Arian characters and language, as well as in Greek, are
supposed by some to be of this king, but
there is nothing known of his reign or character to confirm the supposition. He lost his
throne and life in a contest with Vologeses.

A. D. 52. XXI. ARSACES VOLOGESES, son of Gotarzes,
by a Greek public woman (*pellex*), according
to Tacitus, succeeded. This king warred
with Rome for Armenia, and driving out two
legions, established his brother Tiridates
there. He had a Scythian war also on his

hands in Hyrcania, and is supposed by Professor Lassen to have recovered Kabool and
Kandahar from the Kadphises race of kings,
being identified by the Professor with the
Abagasus, whose coins are found in the Kabool
valley, but this seems very doubtful. Vologeses is the king who addressed Vespasian
assuming the title of king of kings, which
was returned by that Emperor with his own
name only, "Vespasian to Arsaces king of
kings." The reign was happy and glorious,
and of some length.

A.D. 85. XXII. ARSACES ARTABANUS III. son of
Vologeses succeeded, but we know little of
him or of his reign.

A.D. 99. XXII. ARSACES PAKORES. This reign
also was long, but marked by no event of note.
Pakores is declared to have been the friend of
Rome, and ally of Decebalus, king of the
Daci. The coin found of Pakores, with an
Arian legend, may be of this king, and
would show a wide dominion in the East, but
more probably it is the coin of a Satrap who
assumed royalty.

A.D. 115. XXIV. ARSACES KHOSROES (Persian
Khosroo), brother of Pakores succeeded, and
was the cotemporary of Trajan. He defeated
that Emperor's lieutenant Maximus in Mesopotamia, whereupon Trajan, fitting out a large
army, and building boats on the Euphrates,
conquered the entire valley of that river, and of

the Tigris also to the sea, and set up in Seleucia
on the Tigris, another Parthian king, called
by Roman authors Parthanaspatis. On Trajan's death, Khosroes recovered Mesopotamia,
and Adrian granted a peace ceding all the
country east of the Euphrates. This reign also
was long.

A.D. 160.   XXV.   ARSACES VOLOGESES, the eldest
son of Khosroes succeeded. He made peace
and an alliance with the Alani, and cut off
the Roman legions stationed in Armenia. But
the Roman generals, Priscus and Cassius
retrieved affairs in that province, and carrying
the war into Persia, captured Babylon and
Seleucia, in the time of Verus and Antoninus.
The last-named granted a peace after the death
of Verus.

A.D. 195.   XXVI.   ARSACES VOLOGESES III., son of
Sinatrux, brother of the last king succeeded.
This was the king opposed to Severus when
he invaded Mesopotamia, and took Ctesiphon.
He was afterwards involved in a civil war
with Artabanus, during which he died a natural death.

A. D. 215.   XXVII.   ARSACES ARTABANUS becoming
sole king, was involved in a war with Rome;
and Caracalla, soliciting his daughter in marriage, plotted to take him prisoner, or to cut
him off at a conference. Many Parthian
nobles were sacrificed, but Artabanus escaping,
commenced a war of revenge, in which he

made great ravage, and being opposed by
Macrinus, a drawn battle of an entire day
was fought, with great slaughter on both sides.
Artabanus preparing to recommence the battle
next day, was informed of the death of his
enemy Caracalla, and obtained from Macrinus
some concessions which put an end to the war.
Ardeshur Babakan, or Artaxerxes, was a distin-
guished officer of the Parthian army, and an
object of jealousy in consequence. He was
slighted, and revolted, and after three severe
battles, conquered and slew Artabanus, sub-
verting the Arsacidan dynasty, and establishing his own, that of the Sessanians in 235
B.C.; his last victory was gained at Bulkh,
and he was there crowned, according to Persian authority.

Thus closed the Greco-Parthian dominion in
Central Asia, after a continuance of very nearly 500
years. The capital in the time of the Cæsars was
at Seleucia on the Tigris, and the removal from
the original territory of Mushud and Toos was most
probably compulsory, in consequence of the grow-
ing power and encroachments of the Scythians. It
must at any rate have weakened the hold of this
race of kings upon their eastern provinces. The
system of government was purely Asiatic ; that is,
by subordinate satraps, or sovereigns, each pos-
sessing full and absolute authority over the persons
and properties of all the subjects of the state. Bearing this in mind, we have the less reason to wonder

at finding Parthians asserting independence and coining with arrogant titles in Afghanistan ; of this, however, more hereafter.

We have deemed it necessary to premise this brief summary of the history of Parthia, during its transition back from Hellenism to a purely Asiatic sovereignty, and condition of society, because without continual reference to its position and relations with the countries bordering on it, the condition of Bactria, Aria, and of Kabool, *i. e.*, the country of the Kophenes river, would scarcely be intelligible.

We shall now put together what the learning and research of western scholars have extracted from ancient authors, and from modern discoveries, in respect to those more distant regions ; and here we have to remark, that amongst cotemporary writers on this subject, Professor Lassen* only has endeavoured to generalize the data, and to classify the kings, whose names have come to light, systematically by dynasties. Others have been content to treat the subject more strictly numismatically, and to discuss the coins rather than the historical probabilities connected with the names they bear, and Professor Wilson, especially, has preferred that course. There is undoubtedly in Professor Lassen's method something very national and German ; he launches boldly into the wide ocean of conjecture to supply deficiencies in his information, and builds theories regarding his dynasties, nations, and races,

---

* Zur Geschichte der Grechischen Konige in Bactrien, by Christian Lassen. Boun, 1838. (Translated in Calcutta, 1840.)

without any very substantial stratum of authoritative facts for a foundation, and with materials
quarried often in the imagination. The course of
our English professor is the safer for the critic, and
may on that account have more lasting value. He
has ordinarily the support of Mionnet, Visconti,
P. Rochette, and other eminent numismatists, for
the inferences he draws, and assigns dates to the
different kings, of whom no mention is made in
history, upon evidence afforded by the coins in
their execution, or through some similarity of
emblems and symbols with those of other countries, or with one another.

We confess, however, that we incline to adopt
many of Professor Lassen's speculations, theoretical
as they are, and think the plan of systematic
arrangement which he has adopted far preferable
for the general reader. We shall proceed, therefore, to explain the principles of his classification,
noticing the principal differences of opinion between
him and Professor Wilson, and adding, with the information brought to light since the works of both
Professors were written, a theory of our own, in
respect to one of the Scythian dynasties, resuscitated by these discoveries.

Professor Lassen, using as landmarks those kings,
whose names he finds mentioned in ancient authors
with any circumstances to connect them with particular regions, or with settled dates and known
events, arranges the new kings, whose coins have
been recently discovered, on the following principles,

which, whether original or borrowed from preceding antiquarians, are at least rational, and command assent.

First, one or two coins only have yet been found of Theodotus, but these, as well as the coins of Euthydemus, and of Demetrius, the known earliest kings of Bactria and Ariana, resemble the coins of the Seleucidæ, or Greco-Syrian kings; they are of excellent workmanship, with fine heads on the obverse, and some mythological emblem on the reverse, and with superscriptions generally confined to the latter side, in the Greek language only. Such being the character of the earliest coins, any similar that have been, or may be found, with new Greek names and simple titles can, it is assumed, belong only to the same race and period. Coins of Heliocles, Antimachus, Agathocles, and Eucratides, have been discovered, answering precisely to this description; but there is this difference, that of all these kings, there are also coins with bilingual inscriptions, whereas, of the earliest kings, there are none yet found that are not purely and exclusively Greek. These kings, therefore, or some of them, the two last named supposed the earliest, taking up the coinage from their predecessors, in the provinces which used Greek only, may fairly be presumed to have made the change during their reigns, by introducing the new language, also, where it was vernacular, which must have been in some part of their dominions. Their reigns, too, must, it is assumed, have preceded those of kings, of whom

none but bilingual coins exist, unless the latter held
dominion in different territories. The new language
we find called Arian, Arianian, Bactrian, and Kaboo-
lian (we prefer the first of these names), according to
the supposed locality of its native use. All the kings
who adopted it for their coins place it only on the reverse, reserving the original Greek for the obverse,
with the head or bust. Eucratides is a known
king, cotemporary with Mithridates I. of Parthia;
the others above named are new: of them more
hereafter.

Secondly. There are coins with Greek inscriptions only, of inferior workmanship, and with Barbarian names; some of these have pure Greek
titles, as ΣΩΤΗΡ, ΜΕΓΑΣ, ΔΙΚΑΙΟΣ, &c., and some
have both barbarian names and titles. All these
Professor Lassen ascribes to Scythian dynasties,
who are known to have overrun Soghdiana and Bactria in the second century before our era, and subsequently to have established themselves in Afghanistan. The coins of this description of different
types he assigns to different races and periods of
this Scythian dominion, and, in doing so, is compelled to deal largely with theory and conjecture,
seeking supports from Chinese and Mongolian
sources, as well as from classic authors.

Thirdly. By far the largest number of the new
coins found are bilingual, of excellent workmanship.
Many have fine Greek heads, with plain inscriptions on one side, and on the other some type from
Grecian mythology, as Jupiter, Minerva, Hercules,

or the Dioscuri (Castor and Pollux). Some have
a horseman on the obverse, or a Victory with
wings, or an elephant, or a Bactrian camel, and
some have on the reverse a device of this description, and some on both sides; but the kings' names
are in pure Greek, the inscriptions plain, and the
strange language on the reverse having been decyphered, by using the names as a key to the
alphabet, proves to be Sanscrit, or Pracrit, the
vernacular form of Sanscrit, written semitically
from right to left. These bilingual coins, like the
pure Greek coins, are of several races of kings: Of
some both names and titles are pure Greek, with
Arian words, exactly corresponding; of some, the
names are Parthian, and titles Greek, with Arian
inscriptions, not exactly corresponding; of others,
again, the names are barbarian, but titles Greek,
and exactly translated into Arian. But there is a
fourth class, with barbarian names and titles in
scarcely legible Greek characters, and with Arian
inscriptions, not corresponding, and not decypherable, or rather not yet decyphered. All these
belong, of course, to different races and dynasties,
and the perspicacity of the critic is shown in the
arrangement and classification of the names by
these criteria.

Fourthly. There is again another class of coins
of copper, and roughly executed, with Greek inscriptions and names on one side, and on the other
the kings' name, only without any title, in ancient
Sanscrit characters, exactly corresponding with

those of Asoka's inscriptions on the rocks of Girnar
and Cuttack, and on the pillars of Dehli, Bhitari,
and Allahabad. Only two kings, Agathocles and
Pantaleon, are yet known to have coined money
with such inscriptions, and the former coined
also with Greek inscriptions only.

Professor Lassen argues, with great apparent
reason, that, as we find pure Greek to be carried
on through Scythian dynasties, and the first
use of Arian inscriptions to be by Greeks, and
not by Scythians, the new language is not of
Scythian origin: and further, that it was not in
use in the regions of this particular Greco-
Scythian coinage; that is, in Bactria and Soghdiana, the known Greek kings of which, Theodotus, Euthydemus, &c., coined only Greek, like
these Scythians. Further, because the language,
so far as it has yet been decyphered, proves to be
Sanscrit, though written from right to left, he assigns it to the Kabool valley and the Paropamisus,*
which are known to have been peopled from India
before the expedition of Alexander. The coins,
with Sanscrit characters of the age of Asoka, he
assigns to the country immediately bordering on
the Indus, and to a period earlier than that of the
adoption of the Arian language. A peculiar value

* The Paropamisus being peopled from India, may have
received its alphabet from Assyria, which would account for
the language being of Sanscrit, and the alphabet of semitic
origin. In the tombs of Tuscan kings Greek has been found
written in the same manner.

will attach to the bilingual Arian coins, if, through
them, we succeed in completely discovering the
language, of which they are the key, and so obtain,
from inscriptions on rocks and relics, substantial
evidence of dates and circumstances connected with
the dynasties which used it. The late Mr. James
Prinsep, whose perspicacity and laborious study
had previously restored the language of the Indian
kings we read of as corresponding and making
treaties with Seleucus and Antiochus, has the principal merit of using the names found upon these
coins, as a key for the discovery of the Arian
alphabet, and of carrying it further into the titles,
by which the kings who adopted the bilingual form
of coinage chose to distinguish themselves ; but in
these researches he had several competitors, and in
the assignment of values to letters, as well as in the
ascertainment of the proper reading of the epithets
and titles, he was sometimes, as we have before
stated, rivalled, if not anticipated, by the learned of
Europe. Much as has been done, however, in this
particular line, we shall not think that discovery
has reached its limit, until the inscriptions found
in Arian characters upon rocks, and on the relics
of topes and tumuli, are also decyphered ; for it is
through them only that we can hope to obtain a
trustworthy historical record, to confute, or confirm,
the conjectures which, at present, are our only
guide in the dark obscurity produced by the indifference and neglect of western writers. The literature of ancient India has been searched in vain for

facts and circumstances to illustrate this period. Sanscrit books are yet more destitute of historical notices, than those of classic Europe. A ray of doubtful light is, however, cast on the period by Chinese historians, and Professor Lassen has made good use of these authorities in the illustration of his theory of Scythian ascendancy: but it is only a lightening glimmer that we derive from that source, and it may prove deceitful in the deductions and inferences to which he has applied it.

Having noticed that the arrangement of the new kings, and the assignment of dates and territories to them, are built mainly on the varieties of the coins above briefly stated, we shall now follow Professors Lassen and Wilson through their chronological classification, and apply it to the known history of this part of Asia.

B.C. 256. The first THEODOTUS, or Diodotus, on whose coins we find the simple inscription, ΔΙΟΔΟΤΟΥ ΒΑΣΙΛΕΩΣ, is declared by Greek and Latin historians to have asserted his independence at the same time that, or a little before, Arsaces revolted in Parthia. If Strabo is to be believed, who says that Arsaces fled from Bulkh to Parthia, because the rival faction of Theodotus prevailed there, the revolt of Bactria may have been some years antecedent. The reign of Theodotus continued until after Arsaces had conquered Hyrcania, for the latter then feared a confederacy of the Bactrian with the Syrian king; he was,

however, relieved from this fear by the death
of Theodotus, and thereupon entered into strict
alliance with his son and successor of the same
name ; from this circumstance we are led to a
conclusion as to the date of his decease.

B. C. 240. THEODOTUS II. We have no certain
knowledge of the character, actions, or fate
of this king, nor do the few coins yet found
afford any means of distinguishing between
the father and son. The extent of their
dominion is also uncertain. It is said, indeed, that the other Greek colonies of the
further Asia, followed the example set by
Bactria and Parthia : but whether Aria,
Arachotia, and the Paropamisus, including
Kophen, or the Kabool valley, ranged themselves under Theodotus, or chose their separate kings, is nowhere stated. We conclude that Theodotus held dominion over all
the countries east of Parthia, because the
name of no other revolting sovereign is anywhere mentioned, and we know that Arsaces I. had only Parthia and Hyrcania.

B. C. 220. EUTHYDEMUS. The coins have ΒΑΣΙ-
ΛΕΩΣ ΕΥΘΥΔΗΜΟΥ* on the reverse only,
with a Hercules standing, or sitting. The
only other reverse type is the wild horse
of Bactria, with the same inscription. This
king we find established at the time of the
cxpcdition of Antiochus the Great, which was

* See plate, No. 1.

E 2

undertaken in B.C. 212. He does not appear
to have assisted in that king's war with
Arsaces, but after the peace between them, he
met in battle the united Syrian and Parthian
forces, and was defeated. The battle must
have been fought near Merv, where the
ancient Antiochia is supposed to have stood.
Enthydemus fled after it to Ariaspe. The
situation of Hazarasp, across the desert, is
precisely that to which, after such a defeat,
the Bactrian king might be expected to retire.* Euthydemus had there the desert
between him and the conquerors, with Soghdiana and the Scythians for a resource in his
rear. His appeal from that place is said to
have had great weight with Antiochus. He
represented, that it was not he that had
revolted from Syria; but, on the contrary, he
had overpowered and displaced the family
that was guilty of that act. That he person-
ally, therefore, was entitled to favour rather
than enmity. On the other hand, that it was
for the interest of Antiochus as a Greek to
strengthen and support, instead of weakening
him, for that it was as much as the Greeks
could do, to maintain themselves against the
Scythians who had been called in by Arsaces.
That by receiving him into alliance, Antiochus

---

* Strabo says that Arsaces fled in the same direction when
hard pressed by Seleucus Callinicus, and was received and
assisted by the Chorasmeni or tribes of Kharizm.

might restore the Greek dominion over the
whole country held by the first Seleucus,
that is to the Indus, which, if he wasted his
resources in a Bactrian war, he would lose the
opportunity of doing. These arguments,
urged appropriately by the son of Euthydemus,
Demetrius, a handsome youth, who found
immediate favour, prevailed with Antiochus :
and Euthydemus, obtaining favourable terms,
led the Syrian army through Bactria, that is,
by the route north of the mountains to the
Kabool valley, and across the Indus, in B. C.
206. There Antiochus made the peace with
Sophagasenus (Asoka), which we find referred to in the edicts of that sovereign,
gazetted by inscription on rocks and pillars
in various parts of India, in characters exactly
resembling those on the coins of Agathocles.*
In B. C. 205, Antiochus returned by Arachotia
and Karmania, that is, by the route followed
by Craterus when Alexander returned. We do
not find that he met any where with difficulty
or resistance: on the contrary, it is evident that
the Greek colonists of this region regarded
with satisfaction the advent of an army and
king of their own race, and derived strength
and increased authority from their passage

---

* See the translation of these edicts in the journals of the
Asiatic Society, for March, 1838, by James Prinsep. That
on the Girnâr rock specifically names Antiochus (*Antiochia
yóna Raja*), as engaged to use his influence to prevent the
slaughter of animals.

through the country. Professor Lassen supposes, on no ground, however, but that of
probability, that Euthydemus, being left by
Antiochus in possession of Bactria, may then,
or subsequently, have added Kâbool to his
dominions, with Herât, or Aria; and that
Demetrius, to whom Antiochus gave his own
daughter in marriage, was made governor of
Arachotia, and Seestan, or Drangiana. Afterwards, when Antiochus fell into trouble, in
consequence of his Roman war, the Professor
supposes Demetrius to have assumed the regal
title in his father's life-time, and to have
extended his territory by the conquest of
Sindh, Kutch, and Goozrat : for history mentions Demetrius as an Indian conqueror, and
we have good reason to believe that Baroach and
Surat fell at this period under Greek dominion.

B.C. 190. DEMETRIUS,* whose coins have ΔΗΜΗ-
ΤΡΙΟΥ ΒΑΣΙΛΕΩΣ, with more variety than
those of Euthydemus on both obverse and
reverse. Thus the head is sometimes filletted,
and sometimes has a strange elephant head-
cap, and on one coin the elephant's head
stands on the obverse, in place of that of
the king. On the reverse we find Hercules, Apollo, and Minerva all standing, and
on one coin the caduceus of Mercury. The
date of the decease of Euthydemus is not
known. Professor Wilson places it in 190

* See Plates I. and V.

B.C. his date for the accession of Demetrius.
We learn from Justin and other western
historians, that Demetrius, after his father's
death, contended with Eucratides for the
dominion of Bactria, and the latter, being
besieged with a few hundred followers, retrieved
his affairs by his valour and conduct, and
finally overthrew Demetrius, and recovered
his dominions, including India. The passage
contains almost all we know of this king, and
of Eucratides, and shows the latter to have
been cotemporary, in the time of his accession
to power, with Mithridates the first, of Parthia,
the date of the commencement of whose reign,
we have assigned above, in the summary of
Arsacidan kings, to the year 177 B.C. Much
argument, however, is raised upon Justin's
words, which are as follow :—

" Eodem fere tempore, sicuti in Parthis Mithridates, ita in Bactris Eucratides, magni uterque
viri, regna ineunt. Sed Parthorum fortuna
felicior ad summum hoc duce fastigium eos
perduxit : Bactriani autem, per varia bella
jactati, non regnum tantum, verum etiam
libertatem amiserunt. Siquidem Sogdiano-
rum, et Arachotorum, et Drangianorum, Indo-
rumque bellis fatigati, ad postremum ab *inva-
lidioribus* Parthis, velut exsangues, oppressi
sunt. *Multa* tamen Eucratides bella magnâ
virtute gessit, quibus attritus, quum obsidi-
onem Demetrii *regis Indorum* pateretur, cum

trecentis militibus sexaginta millia hostium
assiduis eruptionibus vicit. Quintâ itaque
mense liberatus, Indiam in potestate redegit.
Unde quum se reciperet, a filio, quem socium
regni fecerat, in itinere interficitur; qui,
non dissimulato parricidio, veluti hostem non
patrem interfecisset, et per sanguinem ejus
currum egit, et corpus abjici insepultum
jussit."

B.C. 178. EUKRATIDES. Notwithstanding the above
direct evidence to the cotemporary accession
of Eucratides and Mithridates, there is much
diversity of opinion as to the precise date of
both events. Bayer gives 181 B. c. and he is
followed by Professor Wilson, Visconti 165
B. c., and Professor Lassen takes the mean of
these two, 175 B.c. which brings the date close
to that we have assigned to the Parthian king,
whom, however, there is no ground whatever
for considering to be the elder of the two.
Professor Lassen allows ten years for the wars
with Demetrius, which wore out Eucratides,
and supposes him to have finally triumphed
about the year 165 B. c. then to have made
a separate expedition into India, upon return
from which he was murdered by his son. The
words of Justin, and his designation of king
of the Indians, applied to Demetrius, lead to
the inference, that this siege was endured during operations in that direction. But the
country of the Indians included Kabool and

the Paropamisus, and much territory also to
the west of the Indus river, towards Arachotia;
the expression, therefore, leads to nothing conclusive. Strabo adds to these particulars obtained from Justin, the cession of some provinces of western Bactria to Mithridates by
Eucratides during his difficulties, and confirms the reported manner of his death upon
return from India, and this is all we find in
history about this great king.

The coins* of Eucratides discovered in Bactria
and Afghanistan are very numerous, and the
types and devices are various, betokening a
long and eventful reign. We have some exactly like the coins of Demetrius and Euthydemus, with a filletted head only on one side,
and the Greek inscription on the reverse, with
an Apollo. In these Eucratides is simply styled
king, ΒΑΣΙΛΕΩΣ ΕΥΚΡΑΤΙΔΟΥ. Others have
a helmeted head on the obverse, without any
inscription, and the Dioscuri mounted on the
reverse, with the inscription in Greek, ΒΑΣΙ-
ΛΕΩΣ ΜΕΓΑΛΟΥ ΕΥΚΡΑΤΙΔΟΥ. This de-
vice of the Dioscuri, on their caps, is by far
the most common of those found upon the
coins of Eucratides, and is nearly universal
when the head is helmeted.† Again, we have
the same helmeted head with the Greek in-

* See Plate I.

† Not quite universal. See two coins in the supplemental
plate of Wilson's Ariana Antiqua.

scription round it, and with an Arian inscription round the Dioscuri on the obverse, and
this commonly on square coins, the words in
Arian being *Maharajasa Mahatasa Eukra-
tidasa.* There is, however, one very peculiar
coin,* a tetradrachme, with the head of Eucratides on the obverse, and the words ΕΥΚΡΑ-
ΤΙΔΗΣ ΒΑΣΙΛΕΥΣ ΜΕΓΑΣ in the nominative
case, while on the reverse there are two heads,
male and female, with the words ΗΛΙΟΚΛΕΟΥΣ
ΚΑΙ ΛΑΟΔΙΚΗΣ. Professor Wilson considers
this to be a coin of Heliocles, because of this
genitive case; but much the more natural
construction seems to be, that ΥΙΟΣ is to be
understood, and that the reverse gives the
names of the king's father and mother, neither
of whose heads, be it observed, is filletted, to
denote royalty, and to neither name is there
any title or epithet.

We deduce the following circumstances from these
coins. First. That Eucratides ruled originally in Bactria, succeeding Euthydemus
there, as supposed by Professor Lassen; for we
have only pure Greek coins without the title
of great king, whereas the Arian inscription
is never found without this more ambitious
title. Secondly. That this title of great king
can only have been assumed after, and, perhaps
consequently upon, conquests in, and south

* See Journal of Asiatic Society for July, 1838, page 638;
also the additional plate in Professor Wilson's Ariana Antiqua.

of the Paropamisus, or in Kabool, and that
Eucratides, then first of all the Greeks, coined
with the bilingual Arian inscription. Professor Lassen, indeed, supposes Agathocles to
have been his cotemporary, and to have risen
with him on the death of Euthydemus, establishing himself in Kabool, and in the hills to
the Indus, with possessions across the Hindoo
Koosh, as far as the Oxus, and holding them
until overpowered and driven out by Eucratides. In this case, the priority of bilingual
coinage in this region must be assigned to
Agathocles. But the second language of Agathocles was Sanscrit, of the character used by
Asoka, not Arian, as on the coins of Eucratides ; on which account, it seems not impro-
bable, that Agathocles may have been left by
Antiochus, as governor in Kabool, consequently
upon the cession of some part of that territory
by Asoka, the dominion of Euthydemus, being
confined to the country north of the Hindoo
Koosh. This, however, is only conjectural.
The passage cited from Justin, which speaks of
many wars waged successfully by Eucratides,
bears out the inference that he overpowered
Agathocles. On the other hand, the profusion
in which bilingual coins of Eucratides have
been discovered in various localities, joined
to the comparative rarity of Greek coins,
with the simple title of king, seems to justify
the further inference, that Eucratides obtained

Kabool and the Paropamisus at an early period;
and further, that he must have driven Demetrius into India, and ruled Ariana, or Afghanistan, as well as Bactria and Kabool, some
time before the war in which he endured the
siege of five months, described by Justin, and
ultimately overpowered and destroyed his rival.
Then, at last, he conquered or recovered India,
re-annexing it to his Bactrian and Arianian
dominions, and so became sole king over the
entire territory from Parthia to the Indus,
including the Punjâb and Sindh, but was
not so for any long period ; for all authorities
concur in declaring Eucratides to have met
his death from the hand of his son, when on
his march in return from this Indian expedition. No author, however, mentions either
the son's name, or any circumstances that can
be used to assist in determining the date of
this occurrence. Justin declares the son to
have been associated with his father on the
throne, but we have yet lighted on no coins
to support, or give evidence of such an association ; for the double-headed coin, which
might seem to imply this, has no fillet or
royal insignia, nor title of king, even, for the
head on the reverse.

B.C. 155. HELIOCLES.—ΗΛΙΟΚΛΕΟΥΣ ΒΑΣΙΛΕΩΣ
ΔΙΚΛΙΟΥ. The parricide successor of Eucratides is by some supposed to have borne his

father's name, Eucratides, but Professor Lassen,
following Mionnet, thinks Heliocles the most
probable of the kings yet discovered to have
been this son, and Professor Wilson adopts the
same conclusion, giving 147 B.C. for the date
of his violent accession. The assumption of the
title ΔΙΚΑΙΟΥ by Heliocles, is no obstacle, and
if our interpretation of the double-headed coin
be correct, there is the Grecian, as well as the
Asiatic custom, of naming after the grand-
father, in favor of this supposition. The coins*
of Heliocles are found both pure Greek, and
bilingual, which is against the supposition of
their being coins of the father of Eucratides;
but not so of the son, whose government,
though short, will have extended, like that of
his father, both over Bactria and the Paropamisus, where the Arian language was vernacular.

B. C. 150. ANTIMACHUS. ΑΝΤΙΜΑΧΟΥ ΒΑΣΙΛΕΩΣ,
also ΑΝΤΙΜΑΧΟΥ ΒΑΣΙΛΕΩΣ ΘΕΟΥ, and
ΒΑΣΙΛΕΩΣ ΝΙΚΗΦΟΡΟΥ. The figure on the
reverse of the plain Greek coins is supposed
to be a Neptune, but this seems very doubtful.
Assuming Eucratides to have reigned 25 years,
from 175 B. C. (Professor Lassen's date for his
accession), his death will have occurred in 150
B.C. The Professor, however, gives him a reign
of 15 years only, ending in 160 B.C. Dr.

* Plate, No. II.

Wilson, following Bayer, makes his reign extend from 181 to 147 B.C. P. Rochette makes this reign end in 155 B.C., and we incline to prefer this date, which is a mean of all these opinions. We know that Demetrius Nicator of Syria made his expedition against Parthia in 140 B.C., and was assisted in it by the Greek colonists of Bactria, then recently brought under the yoke of Parthia, which was disliked by them. Professor Lassen's supposition in respect to the date of the death of Eucratides—viz. 160 B.C., gives twenty years, while Bayer and Professor Wilson allow barely seven years for the rule of such other kings, as may have reigned in Bactria after Eucratides, before the period of its subjugation by Mithridates of Parthia; our date, 155 B.C., leaves fifteen years. Assuming, therefore, the coins of purely Greek device, with pure Greek names and titles, to be of Bactrian successors of Eucratides, there are only Heliocles, Antimachus, and Agathocles, who fulfil this condition, and the two former coined with bilingual inscriptions,* that is, Greek and Arian, as well as in Greek only, while the latter coined also with Greek and ancient Sanscrit legends. As he is supposed the earliest, and his case is peculiar, we must here introduce him.

---

* Plate, No. II.

B. C. 190. AGATHOCLES,* ΒΑΣΙΛΕΩΣ ΑΓΑΘΟ-
ΚΛΕΟΥΣ. *Agathoklayaja, Sans.* Professor
Lassen considers this king, as we have before
stated, to be the ruler of Kaboolistan to the
Indus, with possessions across the Hindoo Koosh
to the Oxus, and he supposes him to have been
opposed to Eucratides, and conquered by him.
PANTALEON, who also coined with Greek and
Sanscrit legends, and of whom no coins of
pure Greek device and inscription, or with
Arian characters, have yet been found, he supposes to have succeeded Agathocles in the
country near the Indus, not including Kâbool
or Bulkh, which, from Agathocles had, he
concludes, passed to Eucratides, and his successors. If this supposition be admitted, we
have only Heliocles and Antimachus† for the
period from the death of Eucratides to the conquest of Bactria by Mithridates, and both may
well have reigned in that country and the Paro-

* Agathocles 190 to 165 B.C., Lassen. Professor Wilson
places Agathocles in 135 B.C., but this seems to us to be inconsistent with the character of the pure Greek coins of this king,
and with the simplicity of their style and title. Like Euthydemus and Demetrius, he has no epithet; neither has his supposed successor, Pantaleon, any title or epithet, but ΒΑΣΙΛΕΥΣ.
This circumstance seems strongly in favor of Professor Lassen's
conjecture, for the successors of Eucratides appear all to have
coined with epithets, but none of his predecessors, nor himself.

† Professor Wilson gives 140 B.C. for the date of Antimachus, making him the successor of Heliocles ; but this
would be opposed to the fact of Mithridates' conquest of
Bactria before that date.

pamisus in this interval, for we have no reason
to suppose that either had long reigns. We see
no occasion, therefore, to seek a separate kingdom for Antimachus in Drangiana, and the fact
of his coins being found bilingual also, is against
his being the immediate short-lived successor
of Demetrius in that region, as supposed by
Professor Lassen, for we have no bilingual
coins of Demetrius. It would thus appear
that the order of succession in such parts of
Bactria as had not already been ceded to
Mithridates of Parthia by Eucratides himself,
was, first Heliocles, then Antimachus : The
other Nikator and Nikephorus kings, may then
have maintained a struggle with the Parthian
king in Aria, and the Paropamisus, until 140
B.C. when all were subdued.   Agathocles, however, was by half a century antecedent to these,
and in a different region; viz., in Kabool.
If our supposition be true, that he was the
Governor left by Antiochus in Kabool after
his treaty with Asoka, an earlier date by ten
years, than that of Professor Lassen, might
safely be assigned, for that of his asserting independence, and also for his making conquests
over the Hindoo Koosh, if it be required to
carry him there, in order to account for the
Grecian purity of the silver coins of this king ;
but the early date alone will suffice for this,
for the supposition makes him cotemporary
with Demetrius.

B. C. 195. PANTALEON.* ΒΑΣΙΛΕΩΣ ΠΑΝΤΑ-
ΛΕΟΝΤΟΣ. *Pantalawanta,* Sans.   Pantaleon,
according to our hypothesis, might well be
another Governor appointed by Antiochus to
ceded territory, in which the official language
of Asoka was in use.   He may then have been
overpowered by Agathocles, as probably as by
Eucratides, being the cotemporary, not the
successor of the former.   Both these kings
used the simple title of Basileus, without
epithet or addition of any kind, which, with
the perfect form of their Greek letters, is
an evidence of antiquity.   In their Sanscrit
they gave the names only without any title.

Leaving, for the present, the kings of Bactria,
Kabool, and Aria, whose coinage was Greek only, or
Greek and Sanscrit, we must now bring on the stage
the long list of Greek kings, whose coinage has been
brought to light of pure Greek device, with an Arian
inscription on the reverse, generally round some
deity or object derived from the Grecian mythology.
We have seen that Eucratides was the earliest
of the kings who adopted this bilingual inscription, and we suppose him to have done so,
consequently upon his conquest of the Paropamisus, we know it to have been after his assumption
of the title of Great King.   Upon the death of this
king, his wide dominion is supposed to have been
broken into several independent kingdoms, and the
number of kings, great kings, and kings of kings,

* See Plate II., No. 4.

F

resuscitated by late discoveries, compared with the
known date of Scythian conquest, would seem to
require some such subdivision. Professor Lassen
supposes three kingdoms, besides that of Bactria ;
one eastern under Menander and Apollodotus,
comprehending the Punjâb and valley of the Indus
with Kâbool, and Arachotia, or Kandahar, added in
times of its prosperity. Another western, at Herât
and in Seestân. A third central, of the Paropamisus, which latter region, however, we incline to
give to Bactria, because of the bilingual as well as
pure Greek coins of Heliocles and Antimachus kings
of Bactria. Some such division of Afghânistan,
as is here supposed, has commonly followed the
break up of a dynasty of Afghân kings, and holds
good at present in that country, consequently upon
the dissolution of the monarchy of Ahmed Shah.
The supposition, therefore, is not unreasonable,
though without positive foundation in history.

For the classification, and assignment to these
regions, of the kings resuscitated, we have very
vague materials, or grounds for conjecture. Of
these, the first is the continuance of the same or
similar titles. We have, for instance, a long list of
kings, all assuming the epithet ΣΩΤΗΡ or saviour,
with the simple title of king (ΒΑΣΙΛΕΥΣ), and all
using the Arian as well as Greek character and
language, and not dissimilar devices and emblems
on their coins. It is, hence, fair to presume that
these were all of the same dynasty, though, of
course, the inference is not conclusive, nor indeed

generally admitted. The title ΣΩΤΗΡ is uniformly rendered into Arian by the same word, but it is one of the few that have not been satisfactorily read. The word for king is always Maharâjasa 𐨀, on this all are agreed, but for ΣΩΤΗΡ we have 𐨀, or 𐨀. Mr. James Prinsep read this *Nandatasa.* Professor Wilson reads it but doubtingly *Tadarasa.* Professor Lassen *Tádáro* or *Tádárasa,* for he altered his reading of the ô on learning that Mr. James Prinsep had found the last letter 𐨀 used for s. We incline to a later reading by Lieutenant Cunningham, of the Bengal Engineers, who finding the backward stroke of the first letter to be identical with that used with the k in Eucratides, reads the word *Tradátasa,* thus identifying it more directly with the Sanscrit word Trân, protection. We have the nine following saviour kings:—

B. C. 155.   1. MENANDER.* ΜΕΝΑΝΔΡΟΥ ΒΑΣΙΛΕΩΣ ΣΩΤΗΡΟΣ.
B. C. 135.   2. APOLLODOTUS. ΑΠΟΛΛΟΔΟΤΟΥ ΒΑΣΙΛΕΩΣ ΣΩΤΗΡΟΣ,
                 sometimes also, ΚΑΙ ΦΙΛΟΠΑΤΟΡΟΣ.
             3. DIOMEDES. ΔΙΟΜΗΔΟΥ ΒΑΣΙΛΕΩΣ ΣΩΤΗΡΟΣ.
             4. ZOILUS. ΖΩΙΛΟΥ ΒΑΣΙΛΕΩΣ ΣΩΤΗΡΟΣ.
             5. HIPPOSTRATUS. ΙΠΠΟΣΤΡΑΤΟΥ ΒΑΣΙΛΕΩΣ ΣΩΤΗΡΟΣ.
             6. STRATON. ΣΤΡΑΤΩΝΟΣ ΒΑΣΙΛΕΩΣ ΣΩΤΗΡΟΣ
                 also ΚΑΙ ΕΠΙΦΑΝΟΥΣ.
             7. DIONYSIUS. ΔΙΟΝΥΣΙΟΥ ΒΑΣΙΛΕΩΣ ΣΩΤΗΡΟΣ.
             8. NICIAS. ΝΙΚΙΟΥ ΒΑΣΙΛΕΩΣ ΣΩΤΗΡΟΣ.
B. C. 120.   9. HERMÆUS. ΕΡΜΑΙΟΥ ΒΑΣΙΛΕΩΣ ΣΩΤΗΡΟΣ,
                 (also ΕΡΜΑΙΟΥ ΚΑΙ ΚΑΛΛΙΟΠΗ Σ)

(items 4–8 bracketed as: Cunningham.)

We do not vouch for the order in which these

* See Plates III. and IV. for the coins of these Soter kings, those of Nicias and Dionysius only are wanting, having never yet been published.

kings are ranged, but all have similar titles, and as we have observed, not dissimilar devices on their coins ; those of Hermæus, however, are much less perfect than the others, and on some of his coins the Greek letters are corrupted. As he is the last, the coinage of his name may, probably, have been continued by his barbarous conquerors, until Azes took the Indian title of king of kings, and issued money in his own name : of this more hereafter.

Professor Lassen supposes that these Saviour Kings were all successors of Menander, in the Punjâb, Kâbool, and down the Indus. We have added five new names to the list of kings of this class, known to Professors Lassen and Wilson, all which have been subsequently discovered, and published through the Journal of the Asiatic Society at Calcutta,* by Lieutenant Cunningham of the Bengal Engineers.

Hermæus, the last king of the series, is supposed by Professor Lassen to have been overpowered by Azes, about the year 120 B. c., which, assuming Menander to have succeeded Eucratides in 155 B. c.,† would give only thirty-five years for the

* Journal, 1842, page 130 to 137, vol. xi.

† Professor Wilson gives 126 B. c. for the date of Menander's accession, judging partly from the character of his coins, and partly in order to keep his conquests in India clear of those of Mithridates. This, however, is opposed to the Soter classification, which assumes Menander to have been the founder of a dynasty using that title; and we see no reason for placing so wide an interval between him and Eucratides, whose immediate successor he has heretofore been considered by many critics.

entire series. The coins of all, except of the two first and of Hermæus, are very rare; there is no reason, therefore, to infer that they had long reigns; and, if it were necessary to suppose a division of territory, in order to provide kingdoms for so many, the tract of country assigned to Menander and Apollodotus is wide enough to hold several petty sovereigns during a period of convulsion.

The augmentation of the number of Soter, or Saviour, kings affords, therefore, no argument against Professor Lassen's hypothesis in respect to their connection with the same regions, and the fact of Mithridates II. having penetrated as far as the Indus, is not opposed to the notion, that a Soter Greek sovereign may have held the territory beyond, and there preserved his independence.

Let us now take another series of Greek sovereigns with titles and epithets of a different character. We find three kings with the epithet ΝΙΚΗΦΟΡΟΥ, two with ΑΝΙΚΗΤΟΥ, and one ΝΙΚΑΤΟΡΟΣ, viz.*

I. ANTIMACHUS. ΑΝΤΙΜΑΧΟΥ ΒΑΣΙΛΕΩΣ ΝΙΚΗΦΟΡΟΥ (Arian) *Antima-khasa Maharajasa Jyadharasa.*

II. ARCHELIUS. ΑΡΧΕΛΙΟΥ ΒΑΣΙΛΕΩΣ ΔΙΚΑΙΟΥ ΝΙΚΗΦΟΡΟΥ. (Professor Wilson reads ΑΡΧΕΒΙΟΥ also). (Arian) *Archeliasa Maharajasa Dhamikasa Jyadharasa.*

III. ANTIALCIDES. ΑΝΤΙΑΛΚΙΔΟΥ ΒΑΣΙΛΕΩΣ ΝΙΚΗΦΟΡΟΥ *Antialikidasa Maharajasa Jyadharasa.*

1. LYCIAS. ΛΥΣΙΟΥ ΒΑΣΙΛΕΩΣ ΑΝΙΚΗΤΟΥ *Lisikasa Maharajasa Apati-hatasa.*

II. PHILOXENUS. ΦΙΛΟΞΕΝΟΥ ΒΑΣΙΛΕΩΣ ΑΝΙΚΗΤΟΥ *Pilishinasa Maha-rajasa Apatihatasa.*

I. AMYNTAS. ΑΜΥΝΤΟΥ ΒΑΣΙΛΕΩΣ ΝΙΚΑΤΟΡΟΣ (Arian) *Amitasa Maha-rajasa Jyadharasa.*

---

* See Plate II. for the coins of all these.

We have for these Aria-proper, that is Herât and
Southern Bactria, which we know were conquered
by Mithridates in about 145 B.C. and occasionally
over-run by the Scythians, also Seestân or Drangiana. Antialcides is placed by Professor Lassen in
the Paropamisus and Arachotia, in about 160 B. C.
which is his date for the death of Eucratides, and is
supposed to have been followed there by Lysias,*
while Antimachus, Philoxenus, Archelius, or Archebius, and Amyntas, are by the same Professor assigned to Herât and Drangiana, in the period from
165 to 145 B.C., that is, from the death of Demetrius,
till the conquest of that country by Mithridates.
All this arrangement is arbitrary : we would only
observe, that the tract of country assigned to these
kings being in perpetual war with Scythians, or with
the Parthian king, the Greek colonists, who maintained the struggle with the invaders, may well be
supposed, upon the occasion of some temporary
success, to have taken titles and epithets boastful
of the victory. These kings are all simply styled
ΒΑΣΙΛΕΩΣ, with their distinctive epithets, we
have amongst them no ΜΕΓΑΣ ΒΑΣΙΛΕΥΣ, nor
ΒΑΣΙΛΕΥΣ ΒΑΣΙΛΕΩΝ, king of kings, their territory could, therefore, not have been extensive.

There is again another class of Greek sovereigns,

---

* Professor Wilson gives 174 B. C. for the date of Lysias'
accession ; 135 B.C. for those of Amyntas and Antialcides, and
130 B. C. for that of Philoxenus ; Archebius he brings down to
125-120, B.C. but all these dates rest, like Professor Lassen's,
on conjecture only.

who took peaceful titles, implying the possession of some popular virtue, without claim to the reputation of success in war. They are few in number, and one of them is a queen, viz.—

155 B. C. HELIOCLES. ΗΛΙΟΚΛΕΟΥΣ ΒΑΣΙΛΕΩΣ ΔΙΚΑΙΟΥ, sometimes Greek only, and sometimes with Arian, *Maharajasa Dhamikasa Heliaklyasa.* Plate II. figs. 3 and 5.
TELEPHUS. ΤΗΛΕΦΟΥ ΒΑΣΙΛΕΩΕ ΕΥΕΡΓΕΤΟΥ. (Cunningham.) Arian, *Telephasa, Maharajasa, Sukarmasa.* Plate III. fig. 2.
140 B. C. AGATHOCLEIA. ΑΓΑΘΟΚΛΕΙΑΣ ΒΑΣΙΛΙΣΣΑΣ ΘΕΟΤΡΟΠΟΥ. Arian. *Maharajasa, Midratasa, Mikasaklayasa.* Pl. III. fig. 1.

Heliocles, the supposed parricide successor of Eucratides, has before been adverted to. We have no facts or circumstances of any kind to guide conjecture as to the date or locality of the reigns of the other two. The queen is placed, by Professor Lassen, after Apollodotus and Diomedes, amongst the Indian Soter kings, but merely on conjecture. We would observe, that the Arian inscription marks all these as reigning south of the Paropamisus, while the simple Greek coins of the first-named indicate dominion also in Bactria, and this is all we can venture to infer respecting them.

The above recapitulation of names, disposes of all the mint-possessing kings of Greek name and origin, whose coins have yet come to light. We pretend not to arrange, nor to assign dates and kingdoms to them with any certainty, in the utter want of historical data, or materials of any kind. Of all the kings who followed Eucratides, Menander,

and Apollodotus are the only two whose names
are anywhere mentioned in classic authors, and
they are so only incidentally, and not in a manner to show how they came to power, or where
their capital was situated, or how long, over what
regions, and when they reigned.

All we know for certain is, that all have reigned
at some period of the second century before our
era, in some part of Bactria, Ariana, or the Punjâb. For the style of coinage of each of these
kings it is sufficient to refer to the annexed plates,
in which coins of all will be found, except of
Nicias and Dionysius, which, though reported, have
not yet been published by Captain Cunningham.
The style of execution, types, and emblems upon all
are so entirely and exclusively Greek, that there is
nothing in them to which to draw special attention, excepting the forms of letters in the names
and titles of the Arian superscriptions. As has
before been said, these, after for several years exer-
cising the ingenuity of the learned of Europe and
India, who were long doubtful whether to assign
to them a Syrian, Zend, or Pahlavee origin, were
at length determined to be Sanscrit ; and the value
of each letter has been now ascertained with a pre-
cision and certainty that leaves no doubt, so far
as the interpretation of these particular legends
goes. In the course of years, however, the Arian
alphabet seems to have undergone a change, and
the same forms are not to be recognised in later
coins, nor the same epithets and titles ; and the

inscriptions discovered in topes are all in the less
simple later character, to which we shall come presently. Before dismissing these coins, however,
we must notice that numismatists extract some
evidence as to the locality of mintage from the
devices. Thus, the elephant and elephant's head on
the coins of Demetrius, Menander, and Apollodotus,
and also on those of Lycias and Heliocles, are considered as indicating dominion in India. So the
humped bull of Philoxenus, Diomedes, and others ;
while the wild horse and double-humped camel are
supposed to have exclusive reference to Bactria.
Again, because the coinage of Bactria and Ariana
is derived from that of the Syrian kings, who preceded Theodotus, an argument as to the date of
reigns is sometimes deduced from a comparison of
emblems and devices with those of the Seleucidan
coins, as from the Jupiter in a chair of Hermæus,
which first appeared in Syria on the coins of
Alexander Zebina who died in 123 B.C., and so by
a comparison of titles, as the Theus on the coins of
Antimachus. We attach little value to such evi-
dences, which, at best, are only collateral, and lead
to nothing conclusive. Those, however, who take
delight in them, and think that useful results can
be obtained by such means, will find in the annexed
plates which may be placed alongside of any of
the works already published on Syrian coins, all
the facilities they can desire for making the comparison. We have not, indeed, given every type
of kings like Eucratides and Menander, whose

coins are very various, and have been discovered in great numbers, but a sufficiency of each will be found in these plates to show the style and peculiarities of every one of the kings ; and those who desire fuller evidence, must refer to Professor Wilson, or to the original pages of the Journal of the Asiatic Society of Calcutta. It would be vain, indeed, to endeavour to supersede the necessity for such reference in the case of those who desire thoroughly to investigate the subject.

Of the Greek kings above given, Hermæus is undoubtedly the latest. Of his coins it will be seen, that there are four distinct kinds : and the difference between them is so great, that some have supposed there to have been two, and even three kings of the name. There is first a coin of Hermæus with Kalliope his wife, having a double head on the obverse, and in execution and device in other respects corresponding with the coins of other kings of Greek race. Again similar coins have been found of Hermæus alone, both of silver and copper, with the inscriptions, both Greek and Arian, in characters evidently of the same age as those of other Soter kings. But by far the most frequent coins of Hermæus are of inferior execution, and of copper : and of these there are two classes, one with a sitting Jupiter on the reverse, and the other with a standing Hercules. Both have the king's filleted head on the obverse, with the inscription ΒΑΣΙΛΕΩΣ ΣΩΤΗΡΟΣ ΕΡΜΑΙΟΥ, the name being at the bottom. On the coins with the

type of Hercules, however, there are frequently at
the end of the word ΣΩΤΗΡΟΣ, or its corruption,
ΣΤΗΡΟΣ, the two letters, ΣΥ, the meaning of which
has puzzled every body. Though separated from
the name, which, being at the bottom, commences
from the left, these letters are by many supposed to
be part of it, and Su-Hermæus is accordingly given
as a different king. We prefer to interpret the
ΣΥ as an abbreviation. But the most strange part
of this Hercules coinage is, that the inscription in
Arian on the reverse, round the figure of Hercules,
no longer contains the name of Hermæus, nor the
title Maharaja for king, nor the usual word for
Soter, or saviour. The letters, indeed, are in the
same simple form, with exception to a single, or
doublecross, ─┼─, or ┼┼, which, whether letter, or
abbreviated monogram, or mere mark to shew
where to commence and finish reading the superscription, is still undetermined. The other letters
have all been read, but not with the same certainty
as the simple titles of Hermæus's predecessors.
They prove to be *Dhama*, ┼┼, *rata*, *Kujulakasa
Sabashakha*, *Kadaphasa*, and the self same inscription, verbatim, is found on coins with this Hercules
device, having on the obverse a head like that of
Hermæus, but with the name in Greek letters,
ΧΟΡΣΟ ΚΟΖΟΥΛΟ ΚΑΔΦΙΖΟΥ, and also on coins
with other strange names.

   It would be premature to discuss here the relation
of these barbarians with Hermæus, because we do not
believe Kadphizes, or Kadphises, to have been his

immediate successor. All that we deduce at present
is, that the coinage of Hermæus was carried on long
after his reign had closed, and was taken up, or
suffered, not only by this Kadphises, but by some
Parthians, as by Undopherres, or Gondophares ; for
we find this king, also, coining with an Hermæus-
like obverse, and with the corrupted title of
ΣΤΗΡΟΣ, derived from the Hercules coins of Hermæus, before he took the more ambitious title of
great king of kings. We know, indeed, that in
ancient times mints were not exclusively royal; but
the privilege of coining, and especially of coining
copper, was exercised by every city, enjoying free-
dom or municipal privileges. It will be in some
subordinate mint of this description, that the Hermæus coinage was carried down, until the desire to
gratify a new conqueror, or direct subjection to his
rule, led to the substitution of his name, first in the
vernacular dialect of the reverse, and at last on
both sides of the coin.

We come now to the Scythian kings, who, following the Greeks, adopted their forms of money,
that is, coined similar pieces, with superscriptions
similar, and in the same languages, but inscribed
on them their own names and titles, and varied
the emblems and devices.

B. C. 135. MAUES. ΒΑΣΙΛΕΩΣ ΜΑΥΟΥ; also
    ΒΑΣΙΛΕΩΣ ΒΑΣΙΛΕΩΝ ΜΕΓΑΛΟΥ ΜΑΥΟΥ.
    Rajati-rajasa Mahatasa Máasa. Some of
    the coins of this king are of a different type
    altogether from those of the Greek successors

of Eucratides; but we find him at first coining
with a type and simple inscription exactly
similar to that of Demetrius;* then we find him
bilingual, with the type of Straton and Apollodotus; and at last he comes forth in the full
blaze of barbaric pride, calling himself great
king of kings, and issuing a coin exactly like
that of Azes, the Scythian. From these circumstances we are compelled to assign to him
a date anterior to that conqueror, but so little
antecedent as to be his ally, perhaps to have
called him in to share the spoils of Bactria,
and, after enjoying a short-lived divided sovereignty with him, to have yielded to the
greater authority, and power of his associate.
Our reasons for hazarding this conjecture regarding Maues are the following :—First. The
name is not Greek, neither is it Parthian, nor
Indian ; he was most probably, therefore, a
Scythian, the head of one of the tribes that
broke into Bactria between 150 and 140 B. C.
Secondly. His coining in the Greek style
shows, that he must have been established
somewhere in the first instance by Greek
appointment, or at least with Greek concur-
rence, and the style of his Greek, and the
forms of the letters, indicate an early date for
such establishment. He may, with his tribe,
have sold his services to different Greek sovereigns, or free cities, and so at one time coined

* See Plate IV. figs. 12 and 15.

with only Greek, and at another with Greek and Arian, because occupying territory where one or other form of coinage prevailed. His subsequent association with Azes is proved by the correspondence of his later coins with those of that king ; and, by the extraordinary fact, that a coin with the name of Maues is in the possession of Dr. Swiney, which exactly corresponds in type with that of king Azes, numbered 14 in Plate VII. annexed. Now this coin is very peculiar ; it exhibits the king with a trident, a Tartar weapon of war, setting his foot on a prostrate enemy, on the obverse; and has a figure in the midst of fruit-bearing trees, or shrubs, indicating plenty, on the reverse. It must be evident, that if such a coin was struck and issued at the same time by two kings, each bearing the same titles, it must have been designed and struck to celebrate a joint victory ; perhaps one of the victories in which kings Phrahates and Artabanes of Parthia lost respectively their lives. More of this, when we come to speak of king Azes. We have to remark, that coins of king Maues are rare. James Prinsep knew but of two certain varieties, and a third with a Bactrian wild horse, came to him too late to be drawn and engraved (No. 1, Plate V). Professor Wilson notices seven types of coins of this king, and another has since been discovered by Capt. Cunningham (No. 13, Pl. IV.) There are thus

nine ascertained varieties of coins of Maues ;
but of Azes more than thirty have been found,
and he has twenty-five varieties of monogram.
B. C. 130. AZES. The greatest of Scythians was
evidently king Azes, whose coins we find generally with plain distinct Greek characters on one
side, and with perfect legible Arian on the
other. The titles of this king are uniformly
the same. In Greek ΒΑΣΙΛΕΩΣ ΒΑΣΙΛΕΩΝ
ΜΕΓΑΛΟΥ ΑΖΟΥ. In Arian, *Maharajasa
Raja-Rajasa Mahatasa Ayasa.* The types
of his coins are very various.* We lose altogether the well-executed Greek bust, or head,
but have on one side a horseman, armed with
a spear, or holding out his wrist, in a hawking
attitude : on the other side, male or female
figures of various kinds, not referable to Classic
mythology ; or we have animals on the reverse,
such as the humped bull, the lion or panther,
a horse or elephant, or a Bactrian camel, and
sometimes we find animals on both sides.
Professor Lassen looks upon these varieties as
marking the different provinces subject to
Azes, and both he and Professor Wilson recognise in some of the figures Greek and
Hindoo divinities, but we cannot admit the
likeness. On the coin, for instance, which is
common to Azes and Maues, there is what to
us appears to be the king with a trident, setting

---

* See Plates VI. and VII. engraved by James Prinsep, and
already published in the Journal of the Asiatic Society, vol. IV.

his foot on the neck of a prostrate enemy, on the obverse, with the Greek inscription. This Professor Lassen considers to be a Neptune setting his foot on a swimmer, because of the trident in the hand of the standing figure; while Professor Wilson regards the tridented figure, as Siva, and in the plate of this coin he gives horns to the figure under foot, which we cannot discover on two varieties of the coin, and so constitutes him an Asoor, or devil subdued. The inference, however, that this coin was intended to typify a victory is too obvious not to have struck this Professor, and in that we are agreed. But whatever these figures and the animals on other coins, may be intended to represent, all agree that there is a marked difference between the types and devices of king Azes, and the pure mythological devices of the Greek coins of preceding kings, showing a new dynasty and new race, if not also, as we suppose, a new religion.

Who, then, is this great king of kings, Azes, whose coins are so numerous, and so various? where and when did he live and reign? Professor Wilson inclines to consider him an Indian Boodhist, with a name derived from Sanscrit, meaning "The Unconquered" (*Ajaya*), and assigns him a date only fifty years before our era, making him the successor of Azilises, whom he places ten years earlier. Professor Lassen looks upon Azes as a Sacian

Scythian, who conquered the Kâbool valley in the
time of the second Mithridates, and finally destroyed the kingdom of Menander and Hermæus,
in about 120 B.C. Azilizes, he considers to be the
successor of Azes, and supposes him, with others of
the same dynasty, to have ruled in that quarter, and
in the Punjâb, until defeated by the great Indian king,
Vikramaditya, who, from Oojein, is known to have
extended his empire to Kâbool about 56 B.C. Professor Lassen supports this hypothesis by Chinese
authority, for he finds it recorded in the histories
of that nation, that the Szu Tartars, whom he identifies with the Sacæ, were expelled from the Ili
valley by the Yuetchi, or White Huns, whom he
supposes to be the Tochari,* about the year 150 B.C.
After occupying Tahia, or Soghdiana, for a time,
they are further stated by the Chinese, to have
been driven thence also some years afterwards, and
to have then established themselves in Kipen,†
in which name he recognises the Kophen valley or
Kâboolistan. This is a bold conjecture of Professor
Lassen's, but we incline to think it a happy one, so
far as concerns the date and manner of Scythian

* The name Tochari, or Thogari, is more like that of the
Turks, or of the Yuegurs, who expelled the Yeutchi, and
Professor Wilson recognises the Getæ in the name Yeutchi.

† Professor Wilson places Kipen in Soghdiana on the
authority of the Chinese travellers, who, when entering India
from Balti, state Kipen to be to the North. It does not, however, clearly appear from what point Kipen lay north, and we
incline to take the similarity of name for a proof of identity.

dominion in Kâbool, and susceptible of support
from classic, as well as from Tartar authority.
The name Szu, with its varieties Se, Sai, and
Anszu, may however, as it seems to us, be derived from Azes, or Azou, and be the same as the
Asii and Asiani, rather than as the Sacæ of Strabo
and Justin. Professor Lassen quotes from Strabo the
following passage :—Μαλιστα δε γνωριμοι γεγονασι των
νομαδων, οι τους Ελληνας αφελομενοι την Βακ[ριαννν, 'Ασιοι η*
Ασιανοι, και Τοχαροι, και Σακαραυλοι, κ[α. Now this passage, we think, may be construed thus : " The most
famous and best known of the Nomades, were the
Asii, or Asiani, who took Bactria from the Greeks,
and the Tochari, and Sakarauli," &c., which Asii
and Asiani, we conceive to mean the Scythians of
king *Azes*. This construction seems to us much
supported by the extract from the Prolegomena of
Trogus Pompeius, also cited by the same Professor,
" *Additæ res Scythicæ, reges Tocharorum Asiani,*
&c., which we render ; " to which are added the
affairs of Scythia, and the kings of the Tochari, of
the *Azes race and dynasty.*" The Asii and Asiani
are never mentioned by Herodotus, nor named in
history as a tribe or nation, until we find them the
destroyers of the Greek power in Bactria, and fur-
nishing kings to the Tochari ; nor are they trace-
able after this event as a nation. Not so the Sacæ,
Getæ, and other tribes, the names of which are

* We have adopted here the amended reading of Vaillant,
nAσιανοι for Πασιανοι. The Pasians are never mentioned again,
but the name Asiani is very generally used, as of the same
tribe with the Asii, conquerors of the Greeks in Bactria.

found in various ancient authors of previous and subsequent ages. If, then, the Scythians under Azes are indicated as the Asiani, who overpowered the Grecian dynasties in Soghdiana and Northern Bactria between 140 and 130 b.c., or say about 135, b.c. we must allow for an interruption of these conquests by the Parthian kings, who held sway in Bactria as far as Bulkh, until the defeat and death of kings Phrahates and Artabanes in 130 b.c., after which Mithridates II. made some composition with the invaders; consequently the date assigned by Professor Lassen, viz., 126 b.c., will be nearly the time required for the final establishment of the Scythian dynasty by the conquest of Kâbool : and the series of victories that achieved such a conquest, would justify the great titles assumed by the king after its completion. We have no coins of Azes with less pretension than as " great king of kings," and none without the Arian superscription. This coinage, therefore, followed the expulsion of the Parthians, from Bactria, and the final overthrow of the Greek power in Afghanistan ; but we do not draw from this fact an inference opposed to the supposition, that Azes may himself, in association with king Maues, have been the conqueror of Bactria also.

If, however, the Asii and Asiani are to be understood as meaning the Scythian, or Szu Nomades, who obeyed king Azes, it is clear that he united under him many tribes besides the Tochari and the Sacæ, in like manner as other Tartar conquerors of later day have done. The title "king of kings" is of

G 2

itself evidence of this; the Sacians, therefore, can
have had no exclusive property in such a sovereign,
as supposed by Professor Lassen. Their settlement,
first in the Kâbool valley, and afterwards, consequently upon fresh convulsions, in Seestan, or
Sajistan, is an hypothesis that may or may not be
true, quite independently of the general sovereignty
of king Azes, and his conquest of Kâbool, or the
Kophen valley, in 126 B.C., as stated by Chinese
historians. Let us now see how the existence of
such a sovereignty is supported by other Tartar
authority, than that derived from Chinese history.

Abool Ghâzi Khan's genealogical History of the
Tartars is the only work of the West, in which the
traditions of these Nomade tribes have been collected. We there find, that a king named Oghus
(Ooghooz) Khan, اوغوزخان warred successfully for
a long time against other tribes, until he established amongst them, at last, sufficient authority to
attack Itbarak Khan, of Kashghur, and Khotun.
Being worsted at first, he renewed the war, and in
the end conquering this king also, put him to death.
"Then returning by the frontiers of India towards
Talash, Saram, and Tashkund, he took these places,
and sent his son to reduce Toorkestan and Ande-
jan (on the Jaxartes), which he effected in six
months. Then Oghus Khan advanced towards
Samarkand, and conquered that place, and Bok-
hara. Next he took Bulkh, and in the middle of
winter crossed the mountains to Chor, (Chari-
kar?) suffering much from snow and frost.

Here he wintered, and reviewed his army in the
spring, and then marched against Kâbool, Ghuzni,
and Kashmeer, where reigned a king named Jagma
(Hermæus?), who maintained himself in mountain positions for a year, but was in the end defeated and slain. Oghus Khan then returned to
Samarkand by Budukhshan, and sent an expedition westward against Khorasân, &c."
    Now the line of this series of conquests corres-
ponds exactly, with that required for the overthrow
of the Greek power in Eastern Bactria and Kâbool,
and is quite consistent with the retention by
Mithridates II. of Western Bactria, that is Merv,
Herât and Seestân, with which they would not
interfere. The history proceeds, that advantages
were gained over Parthia afterwards, because of the
king's death, and the nonage of his successor,
which also tallies with the accounts of the con-
fusion in Parthia, and increase of Scythian auda-
city after the death of Mithridates II. The Tartar
tradition, however, gives no help to chronology,
for it assigns to Oghus Khan a reign of 116 years,
and a date four thousand years before Chungeez
Khan, whereas twelve hundred years is a sufficient
period to have intervened between the two. In
support of the hypothesis, that Oghus Khan may
have been the great king of kings, Azes, we have,
besides the similarity of name and of conquests,
a curious coincidence; viz., that the Asii or Attasii,
whom we suppose to be the Azes Nomades, are
called also Augasii by Strabo, and Auzasii by

Ptolemy, who places them in the valley of Kashghur, precisely where Abdool Ghazi Khan says Oghus Khan defeated Itbarak before entering Bactria. In one of these appellatives, we have the name of Oghus transferred to the tribes he ruled, and in the other, that of the Azes of our coins clearly handed down for the same Nomade tribes. We think, consequently, this Tartar tradition, as given by Abdool Ghazi Khan, and confirmed by these names of tribes in Strabo and Ptolemy, affords as good a basis for a theory, in identification of the Azes of our coins, who supplanted the Greek sovereigns of Bactria and Kâbool, as the Chinese, not very distinct account, of the migration of the Szus and Youtchi. The Chinese account is, in fact, not at variance with, but rather supports our theory, especially if we are warranted in considering the name Szu, to be the Chinese corruption of the AZOϓ of our coins, with which it bears a remarkable similarity. Having thus found a place in history for king Azes, let us proceed with his successors.

B. C. 115. AZILISES.—ΒΑΣΙΛΕΩΣ ΒΑΣΙΛΕΩΝ ΜΕΓΑΛΟϓ ΑΖΙΛΙΣΟϓ. *Maharajasa Raja-Rajasa Mahatasa Ayalishisa.**

Azilises coined with the same titles as Azes, and with similar bilingual superscriptions, and devices, and these are continued down to some illegible names,† showing evidently a continuance of the dynasty in the country, where the Arian language was in use along with Greek.

* Plate VII., Nos. 27 and 28.   † Plate V. fig. 2.

On one coin noticed by Professor Wilson, the name of Azes is on the Greek obverse, and Azilises on the Bactrian reverse, which we regard as evidence of a direct succession. Professor Lassen's hypothesis, that the dynasty of Azes ruled in the Punjâb, and Kâbool, until subverted by Indian conquest in the middle of the century before our era, seems rational: and that the successors of Azes had not the same extended sway, nor length of reign, with the founder of the dynasty, is evidenced by the smaller number, and greater uniformity of their coins.

In the summary we have given of the Arsacidan kings, it will be seen, that there was an interregnum of civil war and doubtful sovereignty, after the death of Mithridates II., that is in the early part of the century before our era. At this period we know the Scythians to have overrun Bactria, and there is, as we have shown, every reason to believe that they were established under Azes, and Azilises, in Kâbool and the Punjâb, and perhaps in Arachotia, and the Paropamisus also. We know, moreover, that the Parthian sovereignty was restored with Scythian aid, and had sufficient vitality, to subsist for two centuries and a half more in its western capital on the Tigris. It is, therefore, impossible to suppose that, during this interregnum of anarchy, Parthian satraps yielded every where their dele-gated power, and retired, without a struggle, to make way for Scythians. The more natural sup-

position is, that many asserted, and some maintained, their independence, in the territories over
which they were placed with delegated sovereignty
by Mithridates. To Azes, the great king of kings,
many perhaps yielded a nominal, or real fealty;
and Azilises also may have maintained himself as
general sovereign; but after him, we find Parthians
reappearing with a style of coinage, so nearly resembling that of Azes and Azilises, that we feel
compelled to regard them as successors of these
Scythian kings, and to fix the period from 90 to
60 B. C. for their reigns. Vonones, who, in his
Arian legend, is called Balahara, seems to be the
nearest successor to Azilises. Then we have Spalirisus, then Spalyrius, the brother of the king, and
son of Balahara, according to the Arian legend.
These three Parthians must have reigned in the
Kâbool valley, and Punjâb, for there it is that their
coins are found, and not rarely. We may suppose
them to have made the conquest of Kâbool from
Aria (Herât), or Arachotia, which were more pro-
perly Parthian satrapies; but the style of their
coins forbids our assigning them a later date.

Professor Lassen considers it to be established,
from the little we have of Indian history, that
Vikramadiya, the fabulous hero of that country's
romance, conquered Kâbool about the middle of the
century before our era. We have the date of this
king's reign, from the Sumbut era still current in
India, which is 56 years earlier than our own.
No coins have yet been discovered of Indian type

and superscription, that could reasonably be assigned to a king of Oojein; but there is evidence
of Indian interposition in the affairs of Kâbool, and
the Punjâb. Professor Wilson, indeed, makes
Azes Indian, as we have already noticed, and
finding earrings, and Kshatrya caste-marks, on the
head and bust of the obverse of the coins of the
great Soter Megas, "king of kings," sets him down
also as an Indian. Kadphises, too, coined with
devices of Siva, and the bull, Nandi, in supercession
of his original coinage with the name of Hermæus,
and the Hercules type. This king the Professor also
regards as Indian or Indo-Scythian. Jas. Prinsep,
in one of his papers, threw out the idea that Gondophares might have some connexion with Gandha-
rupa, the father of Vikramaditya, giving to the name
a derivation from ΦΑΡΟΣ *pallium*, meaning the
"wild-ass-skin-cloaked," to connect it with the fable
of that conqueror's parentage. All these theories
are ingenious, and some very plausible; still it is
evident, that we have yet to trace, or verify, Vikramaditya. The fact of the Soter Megas having
coined so largely with a Greek legend only, is conclusive against the notion of his being an Indian.
Both Mr. James Prinsep, and Professor Lassen, indeed, considered it to be established, that this Soter
Megas, king of kings, coined exclusively with a
Greek legend on the reverse, and never with Arian.
The coin, No. 23, plate VII., which has the peculiar
monogram of Soter Megas, ⚕, they assign to Azes,
whose name the former thought he discovered in

the Arian legend. Of this coin there are three perfect specimens in the Masson collection at the India House, and they do not verify the reading of *Ayasa*, for the letters under the standing figure on the reverse. Professor Wilson, who gives two engravings of the same coin, assigns it on this account to Soter Megas, whose inscription, "great saviour king of kings," without any name, is clearly legible on the obverse. This discovery of a Soter Megas coin, so like in type to those of Azes, and with an Arian legend on the reverse, destroys much of the theory, which placed him in Soghdiana and Bactria, at the period when Azes ruled in Kâbool. His Greek is evidently of a later period than that of Azes, Azilises, Onones, Spalirisus, and Spalyrius; but it is purer than that of Undopherres, Abagasus, Abalgasius, and that set of Parthians. We are disposed, on this account, to assign him a date intermediate, that is, cotemporary with Vikramaditya, and anterior to Kadphises, and Kadphes Koranos, and the seat of his power will have been Bactria, Soghdiana, and the Paropamisus. This date for the Soter Megas, king of kings, differs from that assigned to him by Professor Wilson, in so far as it places him after, instead of before, Vonones. This Professor also has reversed the order we have given to Azes, Azilises, Spalyrius, and Spalirisus, besides excluding Vonones from the list. Our classification places them as follows.

B. C. 100. VONONES.* ΒΑΣΙΛΕΩΣ ΒΑΣΙΛΕΩΝ ΜΕ-

* See Plate VIII., figs. 1, 2, and 3.

ΓΑΛΟΥ ΟΝΩΝΟΥ. *Maharajasa Dhamikasa Balaharasa.* It seems to us quite impossible to ascribe this coinage to either of the kings of the name of Vonones, whose names are in the Arsacidan list. He will have been a satrap, therefore, who asserted independence, and created himself a kingdom out of the dominions of Azilises, whose style of coinage, it is evident, that he continued.

B.C. 85. SPALIRISUS.* ΒΑΣΙΛΕΩΣ ΒΑΣΙΛΕΩΝ, ΜΕΓΑΛΟΥ ΠΑΛΙΡΙΣΟΥ. *Maharajasa Mahatakasa Palirishasa.* There is no king on the Arsacidan list, whose name is at all like Spalirisus; there is, therefore, no difficulty in setting him down, as an independent sovereign of Parthian extraction. His name is sometimes read Ipalirisus.

B.C. 75. SPALYPIUS. ΣΠΑΛΥΡΙΟΥ ΔΙΚΑΙΟΥ ΑΔΕΛΦΟΥ ΤΟΥ ΒΑΣΙΛΕΩΣ. *Balahara Putasa Dhamikasa Spalapharmasa.* There are many coins of this Parthian, but none in which he calls himself king. For a long time the legend was read, as of a king Adelphortes, but the Arian confirms the fact, that he was only a vice-regent, son of Vonones, and perhaps brother of Spalirisus.

B.C. 70. The nameless great Soter king,‡ on whose coins we find, in rather corrupt Greek, on the reverse always when there is a bust on the

---

* Plate VIII., fig. 4.   † Plate VIII. fig. 5.
‡ Plate VII., figs. 23 and 26; Plate IX., figs. 1, 2, and 3.

obverse, CΩTHP MEΓAC BACIΛEΥC BACI-
ΛEΩN. Of this king, as before observed,
there are coins with an Arian legend, which
James Prinsep and Professor Lassen ascribed
to Azes. On all we find a peculiar monogram, with three prongs, the purport of which
has not been discovered. With the addition
of a prong, the same monogram was continued in coins of Kadphises, and of the
Kanerkis, but it is not found in those of the
Hercules type, derived from Hermæus. We
consider the Soter Megas to have been cotemporary, but not identified, with Vikramaditya,
and, notwithstanding the ear-rings, we do not
think he is established to have been Indian.

But we have another series of Scythian coins,
with no Arian inscription, and differing in other
respects from those of the Azes dynasty. These
have the name of Kodes, Hyrkodes,* and several
other names, not decypherable, and not of Greek
origin, or extraction, though found written in
Greek characters only, more or less corrupt. Professor Lassen, confining Azes as king of the Szu, or
Sakas, to the Kâbool valley, and Punjâb, upon
Chinese authority, supposes the Tochari tribe to be the
Yeutchi, and places them with their *Asian* kings,
in Upper Bactria and Soghdiana, towards the end
of the second century before Christ, at which period
he gives western Bactria to the second Mithridates.

* See Plate V.

These coins, and others similar, of which the
names have not been made out, but on which
there is no Arian inscription, he assigns to these
Scythians at that period. Professor Wilson, on
the other hand, places Kodes amongst the Indo-
Parthians. We think that the exclusive use
of Greek for the inscriptions, defective as they
are, on these coins, fixes their locality in Bactria
or Soghdiana, north of the Imaus, and Paropamisan range, and precludes the supposition that
they were Indian. But there is nothing what-
soever to guide us, in the assignment of these
coins to any particular race of Scythians, or to any
period of time. The comparative corruption of the
Greek letters leads to the inference, that these
Greek Scythians followed Azes, instead of preceding him, and so, ruling the tribes of Bactria
and Soghdiana, were cotemporary with his direct
successors in Kâbool, and the Punjâb. There is, on
the reverse of the great Saviour's coins, the same
mounted cavalier in a hawking attitude, that we
find on the coins of Azes ; the naked or wild horse
of Bactria, or a horse's head, is the common type of
these unascertained Greco-Scythians, and is an older
device. The title " king of kings" assumed by the
ΣΩΤΗΡ ΜΕΓΑC, and also carried down by the
Kadphises kings, is likewise of later date though indicating extended dominion: the nameless kings,
with Kodes,therefore,although mere local chiefs,such
as now rule at Khoolum, Koondooz, and Bulkh, will
have preceded the conquest of the Punjâb, and Kâbool

by Vikramaditya, whose era, 56 years before Christ,
dates from a victory obtained over Scythians in
the Punjâb. India affords nothing but fables
of the exploits of this great king; but Professor Lassen has discovered, in a passage of the
Periplus, a confirmation of the fact of his conquests,
and general sovereignty ; for, with reference to the
city of Ozene, which can be no other than Oojein,
it is stated, that the ancient royal residence was
there. This, as the Professor pertinently remarks,
can only refer to the reign of Vikramaditya, all
other general sovereigns of India having had their
capitals at Palibothra in Behar, or at Kanouj, and
Hustanapoora, on the Ganges, and Jumna. The
want of coins, or inscriptions, of this Indian king, is
much to be deplored ; the more so, as we have in
the pillar and rock inscriptions of Asoka, his predecessor by a century and a half, such undeniable
evidence in support of what we find recorded of that
king in Boodhist chronicles. A similar much de-
siderated testimony of Vikramadity may eventually
be discovered by the researches of future archæolo-
gists, and after witnessing what has been done in
respect to the great Asoka, we should be wrong
indeed to despair. At present, we can only notice
the hiatus occasioned by this Indian conquest, in
the series of our Arian and Kâboolian dynasties.
The recent numismatic discoveries afford, however, evidence of this Indian conquest, in the
fact, that, after this period, we find Hindoo deities
substituted for those of Grecian mythology, and

most so in the coins of those kings, who are supposed to have followed nearest to his reign. To
these we will now proceed.

Vikramaditya's dominion in the Kâbool valley
cannot have been lasting. His empire in India
even fell to pieces after his decease, and nearly a
century elapsed before Chandrasena restored the
sovereignty of Hindoostan in its unity; his death,
therefore, must have left his trans-Indus conquests
at the mercy of Scythian and Parthian adventurers.
Professor Lassen fixes the rise of Kadphises at this
period ; Professor Wilson places him half a century
later. As we recognize at least three kings of the
Kadaphes, or Kadphises dynasty, their rule in the
Kâbool valley may cover both periods. The earliest
Kadphises, or Kadphizes will, of course, be the king,
whose name is found on the Arian reverse of the
Hermæus coins of Hercules type, and again with
the same reverse, and a head on the obverse, having
the inscription in corrupt Greek, KOPΣOXO,
KOZOTAO, KAΔΦIZOY. At this time the chief
had probably not assumed the regal title ; for we
find neither BAΣIΛEΩΣ on the obverse, nor its corresponding, *Maharajasa,* in the Arian of the reverse.
Further, we find nothing indicative of any settled
religion; for the Hercules worship was readily
borrowed by wild Scythians from the Greeks, as a
mere reverence of physical strength. Tacitus
notices that Gotarzes, of Parthia, took up that
worship from the Scythians ; it was, therefore,
common amongst them. In the district of the

first rise of Kadphises, which we suppose to be the
Kohistan, while Kâbool and its valley were subject
to Indian rule, the chief seems to have retained his
Scythian title, and rude worship of Hercules. Afterwards, overpowering the Indian governors, who followed Vikramaditya in the Kâbool valley, and Punjâb, he, or his descendants, seem to have adopted the
Hindoo religion. For when their power was fully
established, we find the kings, dropping their Scythian style, and coining with the Greek titles of
their predecessors, in their most arrogant form,
viz., ΒΑΣΙΛΕΥΣ ΒΑΣΙΛΕΩΝ ΜΕΓΑS, and ΒΑΣΙ-
ΛΕΥΣ ΒΑΣΙΛΕΩΝ, ΣΩΤΗΡ ΜΕΓΑΣ, and after assuming this lofty title, we find a Kadphises king to
be the first coiner of gold, in which coinage, as well
as in the copper, and silver pieces of the same
type, Siva in the mixed male and female character,
and very generally accompanied by the Bull, Nandi,
is uniformly substituted for the deities of the Grecian mythology. At this time, therefore, the
Hindoo Brahminical religion had become the state
religion of the countries subject to the great king
of kings, Kadphises, consequently upon the complete establishment of his sovereignty, in the place
of the Indian successors of Vikramaditya. In the
time of Augustus Cæsar, a letter in Greek was
received at Rome from a king Porus, on the Indus,
praying for assistance, and good offices. This
Indian king, we conceive, not improbably to be the
Hindoo Raja, expelled by Kadphises, which would
allow a period of half a century for the full growth

of the power of this race of kings. The fast increasing corruption of the Greek letters on the
Kadphises coins, is consistent with the notion of a
gradual rise of power, extending over a period of
this duration, and cotemporaneous with the reign
of Augustus Cæsar ; that is, ending with the commencement of our era.

Professor Lassen, seeking from Chinese history
some means of illustrating the rise of this Kadphises
dynasty, finds it stated that Khioutchi-ouhi, or
Kiutsui-Kio, a Yuchi, or Yeutchi, White Hun
(which race he considers to be the same as the
Tochari, or Turks, but Professor Wilson considers
to be the Getæ), conquered the Szus, or Azes Scythians, in about 40 B.C., and dying at the advanced
age of 84 years, his son Yenkao-ching, prosecuted
his career of victory, and reduced the Indus valley,
and Punjâb to subjection, in about 20 B.C. The
time and circumstances of these conquests correspond exactly with what we suppose to be the career
of the Kadphises kings ; but the names are sadly
metamorphosed, and scarcely recognizable. It is
time, however, to lay before the reader the numismatic testimony that we possess, and which, as before stated, we consider as establishing the existence of three kings of this race.

50 B. C. KORSOKO KOZOULO KADPHISES (Arian)
Dhama ⊦⊣ *rata Kujulakasa Sabashakha?*
Kadaphasa. The inscriptions on these coins
have been ascertained by the collation of many
specimens : we have given two of the most per-

H

fect, in the annexed plates, No. 7, Plate IV.;
and No. 9, Plate IX. The reading of the Arian
inscription is not yet quite conclusive, nor have
we any satisfactory explanation of it. The name,
Kujula Kadphes, seems established, and it is
worthy of remark, that on none of the coins of
Hercules type, is there any monogram, or emblem, to connect the coinage with that of other
known, or supposed, Scythians. With Hermæus alone is there the slighest link of connection, not so with other coins of this name
and race, as will be presently seen.

20 B.C. ZATHOS KADAPHES KHORANOS, ΖΑΘΟΤ,
ΚΑΔΑΦΕΣ ΧΟΡΑΝΟΤ. The Arian legend is
not yet settled, for though many specimens
of this coinage have been discovered, all are
defective at the same part. Like the first
Kadphizes, or Kadphises, this king placed his
head, or bust, on the obverse, with a Greek
legend,* and the head is filletted, to denote
royalty, though the title ΒΑΣΙΛΕΤΣ is wanting. On the reverse is a sitting figure, with
the arm extended, and wearing a loose flowing
Indian dress; but whether the figure is mythological, Hindoo, or Greek, is not apparent.
Professor Lassen inclines to think ΖΑΘΟΣ,
and ΧΟΡΑΝΟΣ, to be titles, but, whether titles,
or names, they clearly distinguish this king
from his predecessor, Korso Kojoules, of the
Hermæus, and Hercules type, besides which,

* See Nos. 4 to 8, Plate IX.

the Zathos coins have on them monograms corresponding exactly with those on the Azes coins, No. 22, Plate VII.; and No. 8, Plate VIII., which would seem to indicate, that the Kadphises rule, under the Zathos sovereign, had been extended over some new district of the kingdom of Azes. It is clear, that the Siva worship had not been yet established as the state religion of this dynasty.

5 B.C. VOHEMO KADPHISES. ΒΑΣΙΛΕΤΣ ΒΑΣΙΛΕΩΝ ΣΩΤΗΡ ΜΕΓΑΣ ΟΟΗΜΟΚΑΔΦΙCHC, sometimes OONMO, and OOKMO, from corruption of the letters. The entire inscription is found on copper coins,* having on the obverse the king, standing, in a Tartar dress, with coat, boots, and cap, his right hand pointing downwards to an altar, or pile of loaves, and having a trident separate on one side, and a club on the other. The reverse has the Siva, and Nandi bull, not mistakeable. One silver coin only of Kadphises has yet been found, having the same inscription omitting the word Soter. The gold coins† of this king, with the same reverse, or with Siva alone, without Nandi, have the bust of the king, with the Tartar cap, or the king sitting on a throne of state, or the king in his chariot drawn by two horses and the Greek legend is simply ΒΑΣΙΛΕΤΣ ΟΟΗΜΟΚΑΔΦΙCHC.

On all the coins, whether of gold, silver, or

* See Plate IX. No. 10.
† See Plate IX. No. 11 ; and Plate X.

copper, which have the title ΒΑΣΙΛΕΥΣ, there is to
be found the monogram, ☆, which corresponds
with the monogram on the coins of the nameless
ΣΩΤΗΡ ΜΕΓΑΣ, except that it has four, instead of
three prongs; and on most of them we find a further monogram, ☆, borrowed from the undecy-
phered coin, given as No. 2, Plate V., which has on
the obverse a mounted warrior, and on the reverse
a Hercules, crowned by two figures, one a winged
victory. The Arian legends, on the reverse of all
the Kadphises coins of this class, have been carefully collated, and contain several new letters
which are variously decyphered. Mr. James Prinsep
read the entire inscription, thus—*Maharajasa
Rajadhi Rajasa Sabatracha ihacha Mahiharasa
dhi Makadphishasa Nandata.* On some coins,
however, he found before the name, *Sabal-
lasa Saviratasa Mahichhitasa,* and on the gold
coins, *Vavahima Kadphisasa,* corresponding with
OOHMO, before the same name in Greek. The
meaning of this legend, as first given, he rendered
" Of the great sovereign, king of kings, everywhere
seizing the earth, Dhima (or Vohima) Kadphises,
the saviour." Professor Lassen adopts this reading,
modified so as to make Vahima always correspond
with the Greek OOHMO. Professor Wilson
reads *Maharajasa Rajadhi Rajasa Sabatraphati-
vahama ha varaha Kapsisasa dhanasa;* but he
is not sure of this reading, and bases it on the
unique silver coin of this king. He does not
attempt the translation.

The only thing certain we gather from these

readings is, that wherever ΒΑΣΙΛΕΥΣ is on the
Greek obverse, Maharaja is to be found in the
Arian legend of the reverse, and not otherwise ;
which seems to prove, that the regal title was not
assumed, until the issue of the gold coinage, with
its corresponding silver, and copper pieces. Korso
Kozoulo, Koranos, and Zathos, therefore, if titles,
were something short of royalty. Assuming the
gold coinage to have been issued about the period
of our era, there are sufficient varieties forthcoming,
to indicate, either one long reign, or a succession of
princes, using similar titles and types, and extending for the period of half a century. Professors
Lassen and Wilson carry the dynasty of Kadphises
through the whole of the first century of our era,
and then consider it to have been overpowered by a
fresh swarm of Scythians, under the Kanerki kings.
There is evidence, however, to a partial restoration
of the Greco-Parthian sovereignty, which, though
not very authentic, is not to be lightly set aside.
Philostratus, in his account of Apollonius Tyaneus,
describes this religious pretender, as leaving the
court of the Parthian king, Bardanes, in order to
travel to India by the northern route, through Bactria, said then to be the easier ; and the journey is
given with such particulars, as must have been the
result of enquiry. Upon crossing the Indus to
Taxila, Apollonius found a king established there,
who conversed with him in Greek, and whose
name was Phrahates. His territory, it is expressly
stated, extended to the passes, from the valley of

Kâbool, into Bactria. Now, though this account of
Apollonius was written in the time of Severus, a
century after his death, and is a tissue of lies, put
together to deceive the world, still, such a fact, as
that a king Phrahates reigned in the Punjâb, and
Kâbool valley, contemporaneously with Bardanes of
Parthia, would not have been stated, if, at the time
of writing the history, such had not been the received notion; and if, in the age of Severus, such
a piece of information was generally received, and
believed, we surely cannot, at this late period, re-
ject it as unfounded. On the contrary, we have in
the coins of Undopherres and Gondophares, who
both called themselves Phrahata in their Arian
legends, a confirmation of the fact that, Phrahates
was not an imaginary king. The corruption of the
Greek legends on the coins of these Parthian kings,
is consistent with the notion, that they followed,
instead of preceding, the Kadphises dynasty; we
incline, therefore, to assign to them a date, in the
middle of the first century of our era, between the
Kadphises, and Kanerki races of kings.

For the reasons thus stated, we suppose, that
during the ascendancy of the Kadphises' kings,
the Greco-Parthian party was not extinguished,
but, holding out in various free cities, and commu-
nities, made terms of submission, abiding their
time to re-assert their independence, and that they
found that time, in the middle of the first century
of our era. From coins, we have the following
kings of kings for this period, and their assumption

of the lofty title of the Parthian king, shows that
their dominion must for the time have been extensive.

A. D. 40. UNDOPHERRES, whom first we find calling
himself ΒΑΣΙΛΕΩΣ ΣΤΗΡΟΣ, in imitation of
the Hercules type coins of Hermæus, and of
Korso Kadphises, (See plate IV., Nos. 8, 9, 10,
and 11,) and afterwards ΒΑΣΙΛΕΩΣ ΒΑΣΙ-
ΛΕΩΝ ΜΕΓΑΛΟΥ, (See plate VIII. Nos. 6 and
7,) Arian, *Maharajasa Raja-rajasa Tradatasa Mahatasa Pharahitasa.** The change of
titles seems clearly to mark this king, as the
founder of his race and dynasty, and he seems
to have retained the title of Saviour in his
Arian legend, after dropping it in the Greek.

A.D. 55. GONDOPHERRES, or GONDOPHARES, who
also called himself king of kings, *Maharaja*
and *Raja-raja,* and took the same Arian name
of Pharahitasa. (See plate VIII. No. 9.)

A. D. 70. ABAGASUS, king of kings. Arian *Abak-
hafasa.* This name is, by Professor Lassen,
supposed to be identical with Vologeses : but
the supposition is built on the idea, that these
Ario-Parthian coins were, of necessity, coins
of Parthian kings, whereas it seems much more
rational to ascribe them to Parthians, who established for themselves a separate and independent sovereignty in Kâbool, and the Para-
pamisus.

A. D. 80. ABALGASIUS. The Greek legends of these

---

* Captain Cunningham reads the name *Undopharasa.*

coins, (Nos. 11 and 12, plate VIII.) are so corrupt, as to be scarcely decypherable. The name, however, is legible, and Captain Cunningham, who published the coins in the Asiatic Journal of Calcutta, made out the Arian legend to be, " *Maharajasa tradatasa Abagasasa Andophara Khudra putrasa.*" "Of the saviour king Abagasus, younger son of Undopherres."

Pakores, king of kings, whose coin,* with bilinqual Greek and Arian legend, was found by Colonel Stacey, in Kandahar, we do not suppose to be of the Undopherres dynasty, the head, and general style, being so very different. The coin may belong to the brother of Vologeses, successor to Gotarzes, for Josephus tells us, that, on this king's first accession, he made over the province of Media (which of course would include Khorasân, and as much of Ariana as belonged at the time to Parthia,) to his younger brother Pakores, and Armenia to another brother Tiridates. There is no reason whatever to suppose that this Pakores had sovereignty in Kâbool, or on the Indus, and he seems not to have held power long, for the general sovereignty of Vologeses was very soon re-established over the entire Parthian dominions.

The above Ario-parthian supposed dynasty brings down the history of Kâbool, and the Punjâb, to the close of the first century of our era, when we find

* See Fig. 13, Plate, No. VIII.

a new race of Scythian kings, issuing gold, and
copper money, of quite a different device, and style,
from any before current. These bear the name of
Kanerkes, at first with the title of ΒΑΣΙΛΕΥΣ ΒΑΣΙ-
ΛΕΩΝ, in the nominative, and the king's name
ΚΑΝΗΡΚΟΥ in the genitive, (See Nos. 12 and 14,
plate VIII.) but afterwards, with the Indian title of
Rao Nano Rao substituted, and the number, and
varieties of the Kanerki coins, betoken a long dominion for kings of the race.

The great peculiarities of this coinage are, first,
that no coin of the Kanerkis has yet been found
bilingual: on all, the only characters are Greek,
but these become at last so corrupt, as to be quite
illegible. Secondly, The king standing, or in
bust to the waist, is given always on the obverse, in
a Tartar or Indian dress, with the name and titles
in a Greek legend round, while on the reverse we
have Mithraic representations of the Sun, or Moon,
with ΗΛΙΟΣ, ΝΑΝΑΙΑ, ΟΚΡΟ, ΜΙΟΡΟ, ΜΑΟ, ΑΘΡΟ,
or some other mystical name of these luminaries,
also in Greek letters: and, Thirdly, upon all the
coins of Kanerki kings, the same monogram �(†)
is found, as was used by the Kadphises dynasty,
after assuming the title of "king of kings," being
borrowed apparently from the nameless Soter Megas.
This would seem to indicate, that the Kanerki dynasty, though interrupted as we suppose by the
intervention of Ario-Parthians, was yet a continuance of the same tribe and nation, as its predecessors of the name of Kadphises. A very few of the

Kanerki coins have been found, with the Siva and Bull device on the reverse, the bull's head being to the left, instead of, as in the coins of Kadphises, to the right. This seems to indicate, that the Hindoo religion was not wholly discountenanced, and rejected. But the Mithraic worship so much predominates, that we are compelled to look upon this latter as the state religion of the Kanerkis, whence derived is still matter for learned discussion and controversy.*

The Kanerki, and Oerki, coins are not sufficiently distinct, to enable us to give, seriatim, a list or catalogue of the different sovereigns. Their power must have continued for more than two centuries, for we find, in the topes that have been opened, Kanerki coins, along with those of Kadphises, and other predecessors of the race, mixed with coins of the Sassanian kings of the third and fourth century of our era. During the entire period of the sovereignty of this race, Greek, corrupt doubtless to the last degree, but still recognisable as Greek, and no other character, is found upon any of its coins. The use of this character does not seem to have ceased with the Kanerkis, for we find the same continued, with a sovereign represented as riding upon an elephant, and called, so far as the name and title can be decyphered, *Rao nana*

* Nanaia is traced to Armenia : In plate V., fig. 7, we give after Wilson, the earliest numismatic evidence of the name and worship. The name round the bust of the obverse is so far lost, that we discover only that it begins with D. and ends with BISES, which shows it to be Persian.

Rao Kenorano. See plate IX., No. 13, and plate XII., 10 to 15.

After this, the Greek characters yielded to Sanscrit, and we give two of the plates prepared by Mr. James Prinsep, purposely to show, how the style and device, of the gold coinage especially, both of Kadphises, and the Kanerkis, was carried on till it grew more and more corrupt, and was at last entirely lost, through the deterioration of art, under the princes of Hindoo race, who succeeded to the more energetic Greeks and Scythians.

Professor Wilson has added to his work notices of the Sassanian, and of Hindoo, and early Mahomedan coins, found in Afghanistan and Upper India. These form a separate subject, with which at present we have nothing to do; but before concluding, we would offer a few more observations regarding the language found upon the new coins, which we have called Arian, and not Bactrian, because there is no evidence of its being the language of the countries watered by the Oxus and Jaxartes.

Although the Greek characters outlived the Arian, upon the money of the Punjâb, and of the Kâbool valley, we have proof in the Arian inscriptions, found on the stones and relics of topes in both regions, that Arian only was the written language of general use, when Greek was quite extinct.

This language was adopted, first by the Greek kings, from Eucratides down to Hermæus, it was then taken up by the Scythians, who crossed the Paropamisus, Imaus, or Hindoo Koosh, and

also by Parthians, who asserted their independence in Afghanistan : we conclude, therefore,
it must have been the vernacular language of
the Paropamisan range, of Kâbool, and perhaps
of Herât, and Kandahar; we find it also in the
topes of Manikyala in the Punjâb. Now the first
thing to be observed of the language is, that,
unlike both Greek and Sanscrit, it is written semitically from right to left. But while the art of
writing was in its infancy, and each character had
a separate and distinct form, never joined into a
running hand, it mattered little whether the characters were placed in one order, or in the other. We
know that the earliest Greek was written alter-
nately, as a plough is driven, and the tombs of
Tuscan kings, recently opened in Italy, contain
inscriptions in Greek characters, written like the
Arian from right to left. The Mongolians, also, who
adopted the Syrian alphabet, write it in lines
downwards like the Chinese: consequently, as
the Arian written characters are always found
with the letters disjoined, in a primitive form,
we are not disposed, on account of the order of
arrangement, to conclude that the language has a
semitic origin, or any close affinity with the languages of that class. We find, on the contrary,
that all the Arian words yet read, which represent
epithets, or titles, such as the words for "king," for
"saviour," for "just," "illustrious," "unconquered,"
" victorious," &c. are pure Sanscrit, meaning the
same thing precisely in that language.

For ΒΑΣΙΛΕΩΣ   we have   *Maharajasa.*
ΜΕΓΑΛΟΥ   *Mahatasa.*
ΒΑΣΙΛΕΩΣ ΒΑΣΙΛΕΩΝ   *Rajadirajasa.*
ΔΙΚΑΙΟΥ   *Dhamikasa.*
ΝΙΧΗΦΟΡΟΥ   *Jyadharasa.*
ΕΠΙΦΑΝΟΥΣ   *Tejamasa.*
ΑΝΙΚΗΤΟΥ   *Apatihatasa.*
For Son   *Putasa, &c. &c.**

This is evidence of very close affinity with Sanscrit, and leads to the hope that by a further use of
the coins, as a key for settling the alphabet, the
dialects of Sanscrit, and the Pooshtoo especially,
may be applied, to the complete decyphering, and
translation of the inscriptions in Arian characters,
which have been found on the relics in topes,
and on rocks, and other remains of the period of
its use.   Fac-similes of several of these inscriptions
have been made, and are now in the hands of
Professor Lassen, from whose learning and ingenuity we hope the best result.   We know that this
work occupied the latest attention of Mr. James
Prinsep, who was confident, that through the
coins, the language being ascertained to be of
Sanscrit origin, a sufficient clue existed for the
complete development of the antiquarian treasures
locked up in the inscriptions ; indeed, that he
considered himself to have already mastered the
first difficulties of decyphering them, and to be in
progress towards the full ascertainment of the
meaning of one at least, if not of two of these
inscriptions.

* See Plate XIII. for the forms of letters.

The work he left incomplete, remains to be accomplished by those who continue to feel interest, and to give attention to these researches, and we look to Professor Lassen, in particular, for an early solution through these inscriptions, of the problems, he has himself so largely raised, in respect to the history and antiquities of the Paropamisan regions.

A further remark we have to make in respect to this Arian language, is, that it seems to have superseded the ancient Sanscrit of the days of Asoka, which was adopted by Agathocles and Pantaleon, the first of whom we know, from the pure Greek style of his other coins, to be one of the earliest of the Grecian kings. If these two kings had not found the Sanscrit language in use, they would scarcely have placed it on their coins. After them, however, the Sanscrit characters were entirely disused. Menander, the known Indian conqueror, never seems to have adopted, or at least to have coined with, the language of Asoka: from which circumstance we infer, that the characters on the coins of Agathocles and Pantaleon were not vernacular, but had been introduced by the Indian sovereigns, who, following the first Chandra Goopta, retained dominion over the provinces ceded by the first Seleucus, until they were restored by Asoka to the Great Antiochus. This hypothesis only will explain, both the adoption of Sanscrit by the governors left by Antiochus in those provinces, and the early discontinuance of the character.

Again, Arian characters only are found on the

vases, relics, and stones, discovered on excavating
the tumuli, or topes, as well of the Punjâb, as of
Jelâlabad, and Kâbool. This seems to prove, that at
the time of the erection of these topes, the Arian
was not only the vernacular language of the dis-
tricts where they stand, but the language also of
the priests, and people concerned in preparing the
vases, and articles used in the funeral obsequies of
the great. If Brahman priests or Boodhist Sra-
manas had been employed, they assuredly would
have used the characters, and language of India,
viz. those of the coins of Agathocles, and Pantaleon,
already once before introduced into these regions.
Scythian priests, again, would have brought the
forms of writing, in use beyond the Jaxartes, and
Belout Tag mountains. And, as Greek was always,
so long as it lasted, the more honored language,
being that found on the obverse of the coins, it is
difficult to understand, why the same language
should not have been used, in preference to the
Arian, for inscriptions on the funeral paraphernalia.
All these are questions, which the decyphering of a
few of the inscriptions will set for ever at rest.

In the hope of drawing more general attention
to them, and perhaps of eliciting a successful dis-
play of ingenuity, in quarters, where the material,
upon which to exercise it, might otherwise be wanting, we give in two separate plates,* transcripts of
two Arian inscriptions, taken with great care, for

* Plates XVI. and XVII.

submission to the late Mr. James Prinsep. These
are the inscriptions referred to in the last paper he
wrote upon Bactrian relics, which was published
in the Journal of the Asiatic Society, for July, 1838.
In his note book, is an analysis of one of them,
and tentative readings of both, which we also sub-
mit to help the student, who may devote himself
to the task of decyphering them. We have only
one wish—to see the end attained, to see extracted
from these inscriptions, some undeniable evidence,
in support, or confutation of the conjectures, we
have here put together; and so to obtain for all
time, a record of facts and circumstances, that may
be added confidently to the historical remains, of
ages and of regions, which for many reasons are
objects of interest, and of increasing curiosity.

In order that nothing may be wanting to those
who undertake the decyphering of these inscriptions, we have judged it right, before bringing these
pages to a conclusion, to reprint, from the Journal
of the Asiatic Society of Calcutta, the substance of
General Court's report of his finding that of Manikyala, which is evidently the fullest, and most
important, in one of the topes or tumuli he there
opened. We add also, an account, with drawings,
of the relics, previously obtained by General Ventura
in the larger tope, he had opened some time before
in the same vicinity, upon which also there are inscriptions in the same Arian characters. The possession of the copper plates of these latter, prepared
by Mr. James Prinsep for his Journal, enables us

to give the whole complete. But we have to point out, that when first these relics came to hand, the Arian characters were quite unknown. They had not then been ascertained, and decyphered, by means of the bilingual Greek and Arian coins. It hence happened, that in the plate of General Ventura's relics, published in the Journal, the Arian inscriptions were given with the wrong side uppermost. Those obtained from Mr. Masson, having been so forwarded, led to the others also being similarly transcribed. In the present plate we have corrected this error.

The following is an abstract of General Court's description of Manikyala, and of his examination of the topes there.

Manikyala is the name of a small village situated on the high road from Attok to Lahore, a little more than half-way between the place first named, and the city of Jhilum. It is built on the ruins of a very ancient city of unknown origin; but the geographical position of the ruins, and particularly the abundance of coins found in them, affords the presumption that this city must have been the capital of all the country between the Indus and Hydaspes, a country which the ancients knew by the name of Taxila, and of which frequent mention is made in the history of Alexander.

There is at Manikyala a vast and massive cupola of great antiquity. It is visible at a considerable distance, having a height of about 80 feet, with a circumference of 310 or 320 feet. It is

I

solidly built of quarried stones with lime cement. The outer layer is of sandstone. In the interior, the masonry is of granite and sandstone, mixed with a porous limestone. The outer surface is now so worn and furrowed, that it is not difficult to climb to the summit, which, when the building was new, must have been impossible. The architecture is simple; the only ornament is a range of small columns near the base, having ram's heads for their capitals, which, however, are now scarcely distinguishable. This is the tope opened by General Ventura.

Monuments of the same kind are met with at Rawul Pindi (in the Punjâb), in the Huzâra country west of Kâbool, at Jelâlabad (many of which have since been opened by Mr. Masson, and the relics of which are reported in Professor Wilson's Ariana Antiqua), also at Lagman, Kâbool, and Bâmean, and in the Khybur Pass.

Amongst the ruins of Manikyala, are fifteen other cupolas, smaller than that above described. These were all opened by General Court, and one in particular, distant about a cannon-shot to the N. N. E. of the present village, afforded rich materials. Amongst the coins, were some genuine Roman pieces,* and the stone which *served as a covering to the niche, which contained the relics, was*

---

* See Journal of Asiatic Society, for November, 1834, for plates of these Roman coins, which are of the first Cæsars, and of the Triumvirate.

found sculptured all over with inscriptions. It is from a wax impression of these inscriptions, that the annexed lithographic plate was prepared carefully by the late Mr. James Prinsep.

The cupola of the tope, which contained these relics, was so dilapidated, as almost to have escaped notice. Its height originally may have been 60 or 70 feet. It was pierced by General Court, from the centre of the summit, with a hole of about 20 feet diameter. The materials were a coarse concrete, very porous. The first discovery was of four copper coins, three feet only from the upper surface, one is of Kadphises, the other three of Kanerkes. Below this were large blocks, which made it difficult to penetrate the masonry. On working ten feet through these, a rectangular cell was found, built with dressed stones firmly united with mortar. The cell was in the form of a paralellogram, having its four sides corresponding with the four cardinal points, and at the top was one massive slab, upon which were the inscriptions. In the centre of the cell stood a copper urn, round which were placed symmetrically, eight medals of copper, much corroded, but with sufficient left of the stamp and device, to show two to be of the Kadphises type, and the rest Kanerkis. The urn was carefully enveloped in a wrapper of white linen, adhering tightly, but which fell to shreds when the urn was handled. In the copper urn was a smaller silver one, the space being filled with an earthy paste impregnated with verdigris and still moist; there was found in this pasty substance, a thread, or string, tied in a knot, which also, on being handled, was reduced to powder. The silver of this interior vase was quite corroded, so as to break into pieces.* Within it was a much smaller vessel of gold, bedded in the same brown paste, along with seven silver coins, all evidently Roman. The gold vessel contained four small gold coins of Greco-Scythian type, all Kanerkis, and two precious stones, with four decayed pearls bored as for ear-rings.

The discovery of the inscription led to a re-examination of the opening, made by General Ventura in the large tope at the same place, but no stone could be found there with any trace of letters, nor were inscriptions found in other topes opened at Manikyala by General Court.

General Ventura's operations for opening the large tope, were commenced on the 27th of April, 1830, at the bottom of the cupola on the south side, but, finding there nothing but rubbish, he recommenced from the summit. At the depth of three feet, he met with six coins, and after penetrating to twelve feet, the building was of solid large quarried stones, through which the work was carried on with difficulty. On reaching ten feet below the surface of this masonry, another coin was found in a clod of earth, and at the depth of twenty feet, one

---

* The General probably mistook lead, or tin, for silver, for the corrosion of silver, when the copper was nearly perfect, is scarcely intelligible.

silver and six copper coins.* Two days afterwards
the workmen reached a box of iron or copper, which
was broken by their pickaxes, and contained a
small box of pure gold, (Fig. 1. Plate XIV.) in the
centre of which was an opal. The box contained
a gold coin, weighing 122 grains, of the Kanerki
race, the Greek very corrupt, (Fig. 2. Plate
XIV.) also a gold seal-ring set with a sapphire,
having a Pahlavee inscription, (Fig. 3. Plate XIV.)
a small bit of ruby (Balas or Budukshany), three
small silver coins without stamp, a Sassanian silver
coin, (Fig. 8. Plate XIV.) of a type corresponding
with that assigned by Longperier to king Sarbaraz,
who reigned only forty days, and on the margin of
which both he and Professor Wilson read the
Mahommedan Bismillah. Mr. James Prinsep considered this to be a coin of Sapor II. because of the
crescent and wings at the top of the crown, or head
dress, but the subject was not then so well understood as at present. There were also found, two
other Sassanian coins, of types not given in Longperier, but having Deva-nagri legends, (Nos. 10, 11.
Plate XIV.) From a more perfect specimen of No.
11, obtained through Sir A. Burnes, its Deva-nagri
legend was read by Mr. James Prinsep thus—*Svi
hitivira Airan cha parameswara sri Vahitigan deva-*

* General Ventura unfortunately mixed these coins, so as to
be unable afterwards to discriminate, which were found at
each of these different depths, but all were apparently of the
same age as the Sassanian coins, that is as late as the fifth
century.

janita. A rude silver coin of India, corrupted from the Kanerki type, and evidencing a very modern date for this deposit, completed the list of articles belonging to it.

Not satisfied with the discovery thus made, General Ventura proceeded with the perforation, until on the 25th of May it had been carried to the depth of forty-five feet. There on lifting a large quarried stone, a similar was found below, with a hole excavated in its centre, wherein was deposited a copper box, (Fig. 12. Plate XIV.) with the lid decayed, and having inside a piece of cloth, (Fig. 13), a chrystal drop, (Fig. 14), and a small cylinder of pure gold (Fig. 15.) Carrying the excavation yet further, a copper coin was found at the depth of fifty-four feet, and three more Sassanian coins, with some trifling articles, all much corroded.

On the last day of May, at the depth of sixty-four feet, an immense slab was reached, which laid open a chamber, built up with stone and cement. In this was a box of copper, (Fig. 19. Plate XV.) filled with a brown liquid substance, which upon analysis was found to contain decomposed animal substance. Inside of this, was a turned brass box, well preserved, and showing still the marks of the turning tool, but with the top broken off; on the lid of the box was an Arian inscription, punctured circularly as shown in Fig. 20. Plate XV. In the brass box, were five copper coins of the Kanerki, and Kenorano type (Figs. 28 to 32), and a cylinder of pure gold, all bedded in the liquid brown substance above mentioned. The cylinder opened with a lid fitting inwards, and contained some fragments of amber, or glass, and a small piece of string, (Fig. 23. Plate XV.) together with a small gold coin (Fig. 24. Plate XV.) weighing thirty grains, (a semi-drachma), of the type Kanerki Koranos, also a plain disc of silver, bearing two lines of Arian characters deeply cut, (Fig. 26. Plate XV.) A small piece of gold, (Fig. 25. Plate XV.) complete the list of these relics, all which were presented by General Ventura to Mr. James Prinsep, and now form part of the cabinet belonging to his estate.

General Ventura carried the excavation afterwards to the foundation below the masonry, but found nothing more: we have, therefore, in the above relics, the first and most ancient deposit of this tope. The coins forbid our ascribing it to a period earlier than the reign of Kenorano, the latest of the Kanerkis, if he was at all of that race: We find, however, that while the coins have still the Greek legends, the inscriptions on all the relics are exclusively Arian. This is the case as well in this tope, as in that afterwards opened by General Court.

It is probable that General Court's was the more ancient of the two, for in that we find Roman coins mixed with those of Kanerki and Kadphises, but none of Kenorano, the Elephant mounted king, and none Sassanian. In both, however, the in-

scriptions are all in the same character: and, with
this statement of the circumstances attending their
discovery, we commit them again to the ingenuity and research of the learned. They have
already been published, with the same plates, in
the pages of the Journal of the Asiatic Society of
Calcutta.

Mr. Masson, excited by the interest evinced regarding the relics obtained from the topes of Manikyala, opened as we have before stated, very
many at Daranta, and Hidda, near Jelâlabad,
and in other parts of the Kâbool valley. The
particulars of his discoveries will be found given
at length, in Professor Wilson's Ariana Antiqua,
to which we refer our readers. Two inscriptions,
however, found on a cylinder extracted by Mr. Masson, from a tope at Jelâlabad, are given in Plate
XV., as published originally in Calcutta, along with
the Manikyala relics. They were forwarded by
this gentleman to Calcutta in 1834, with the first
notice of his discoveries in this branch of archæology. Our repetition of the publication will not,
therefore, we feel assured, be regarded as an usur-
pation of his right in them; but it is proper to
make the acknowledgment, that these are a part of
his labours, and as such will be found also in the
pages of Professor Wilson.

One thing seems to be proved by these late
searches into the interior of the topes or tumuli of
the Punjâb and Kâbool valley ; namely, that they
are sepulchral monuments, erected for the deposit

and preservation of the urns, in which the ashes, and unconsumed remains of persons of distinction were collected, after burning their bodies on the funeral pile. Arrian expressly tells us that it was not the custom in India to erect expensive tombs to kings ; but we know that eight stupas, or topes, nearly similar in form to these, were erected over the remains of Sakhya Boodh, after his body had been burnt in Behar. The inscription on the slab, which closed the chamber of the tope, opened by General Court, contains letters, which are unmistakeably " *Maharajasa,*" being identical with those letters on the bilingual coins. That tope, therefore, must have contained the remains of a king, and we infer, that he was a king of the Kanerki race, from the coins of this type being the latest found in them. But it is singular, that the gold coins found in the interior cylinder, have neither the title of Maharaja, nor its Greek equivalent ΒΑΣΙΛΕΥΣ, Rao nano rao, being the words of their legend, which are supposed later titles. This adds to the curiosity that must be felt, to decypher, and settle the interpretation of the entire inscription, in which we recognise the earlier title. The coins and relics found at different depths, above the lower chamber in both topes, may, not improbably, be similar remains of members of the same family, who died while the topes were in course of erection, or not very long after their completion. The deposit of coins, made with each sepulchral urn, seems to be a custom derived from the Greeks, to provide the soul of the deceased with Charon's

fee.   But we have yet no evidence that the
erection of topes was a practice of the Greek colonists, for, in no single tope yet opened, has there
been any Greek inscription found, or coin of a
Grecian king, or other relic referable to the
known institutions of that race.   The topes seem
to be of Scythian origin, and are in all respects
analogous to the mounds, and tumuli, left by
invaders of the Scythian and Gothic race, in
all parts of the world, overrun, or traversed by
them.   But it seems strange, that, while we know
that the coins of Menander and Apollodotus formed
the general currency of these regions, Roman
coins should be sought out to be deposited with the
inmost relics, to the exclusion of these.

Kupoordigiri, where the other Arian inscription
referred to above was found, is a town in the midst
of ruins, situated about forty miles N. E. from Peshawur.   The inscription was on a large stone, from
which a part had been broken off.   Sir A. Burnes
furnished, together with a copy made from sight,
an impression taken from the stone itself with wet
paper and lamp black.   It is from these collated,
that the copy was made, which has been found in
Mr. James Prinsep's Note-book, and from which
Plate XVII. is taken.   On the plate of the Kupour-
digiri inscription, we give an   analysis of that
of Manikyala, made by Mr. James Prinsep, and
found also in his Note-book.   From the same source,
we give two tentative readings of both the Kupoordigiri, and Manikyala inscriptions.   These were

found imperfect, and cannot be considered as the final readings, which Mr. James Prinsep contemplated publishing with an interpretation, but was prevented executing, by the attack of paralysis, which terminated in his decease. We give them only as materials to help future labourers in the same field.

Tentative Readings of Kupoordigiri inscription, Plate XVII.

First—Parshitama ja ra ka dhi — rajasa
                               tee
        Sataya sa tetáre sarke u chethiya,
                bhu
        —Tala karmma diga keta bhute fantesa tata yeta khsa
                tin
        Antiripale pidhi n varsa khatlesuram bha kata
        Sha ra kiti vrija vadhi de ke riti di ya pade shu.

Second—Aparajita matava
        Satadasa tituriso juke sidhi ja—
        Jau a tra ta mmari da keta tiphira ti sa tuta ji tanha
        Arati pala pitira va jusa ra te sa ra mu ka ta
        Sata ki ti vuta vari de ke ritari jaupatâ.

Tentative Readings of part of Manikyala Inscription, Plate XVI.

First—   gh?   ba   f
        Keraladhara rusti sa anapa viha sati va
                * 120
        Sta CXX swan apurbeswa Maharajasa kane
        Shsm
        State vusta khata d — sa tatbakatala
                sana
        Vacha safa — ai sisa mudra pasa
        Hâra i dwasa dasa apakha niti haja
        Nana i biana — kestata dwi dra wuta.

* Qy. borrowed from the Romans?

Second—Pora ra na ra rudhi sa Afapa viaza ma va
      — 220 vana putha ka Maharajasa kani
      Ksha rashva shr Khuda ra cha o dadu ka lala
      Va — yaphana — shisa mutra pasa
                         ja
      Hata e rt sa dasa apakha pheti ha va
      Tratra — anare —

The manuscript gives no more, and there is no attempt at translation.

FINIS.

W. Lewis and Son, Printers, 21, Finch-lane, Cornhill.

EUTHYDEMUS, 220-180, B.C.

Plate 1.

DEMETRIUS, 200-165, B.C.

EUCRATIDES THE GREAT, 180-160, B.C.

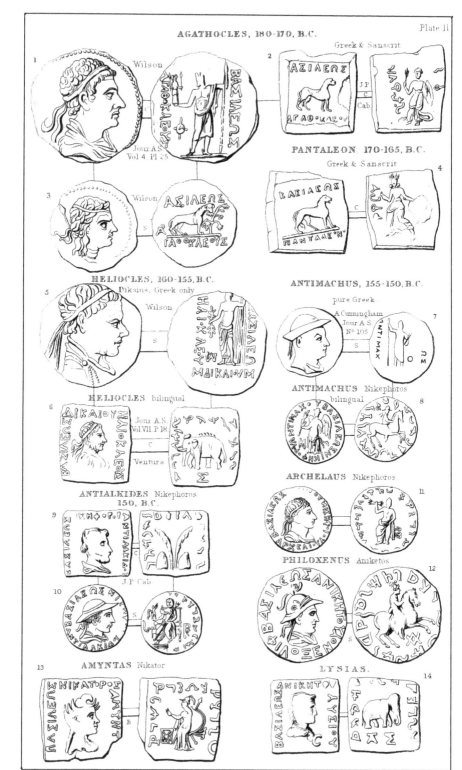

AGATHOCLES, 180-170, B.C.

Greek & Sanscrit

PANTALEON, 170-165, B.C.

Greek & Sanscrit

HELIOCLES, 160-155, B.C.
Dikaius, Greek only

ANTIMACHUS, 155-150, B.C.

pure Greek

HELIOCLES bilingual

ANTIMACHUS Nikephoros
bilingual

ARCHELAUS Nikephoros

ANTIALKIDES Nikephoros
150, B.C.

PHILOXENUS Aniketos

AMYNTAS Nikator

LYSIAS.

Plate II

QUEEN AGATHOCLEIA.   TELEPHI'S.   Plate III

SOTER KINGS, 160-120, B.C.

MENANDER.

APOLLODOTUS.

DIOMEDES.   ZOILUS.

STRATON.

G. Barclay sc

Plate IV

HIPPOSTRATUS SOTER.
Cunningham.
As Jour Vol XI

HERMÆUS & CALLIOPE.

HERMÆUS SOTER.

HERMÆUS SOTER.
J P Cab
As Soc Jour
Vol IV Pl 24

KORSO KOSOULO KADPHIZOU.

UNDOPHERRES SOTER.
J P Cab
As Soc Jour
Vol IV Pl 24.

J P Cab
Jour
Vol IV
Pl 25.

MAUES, KING, 135, B.C.
Cunningham
As Jo
Vol XI

MAUES, King of Kings 130, B.C.
As Jour Vol VII Pl 28 Ventura

DEMETRIUS.
As Jour
Vol XI
Pl 1

G. Barclay sc

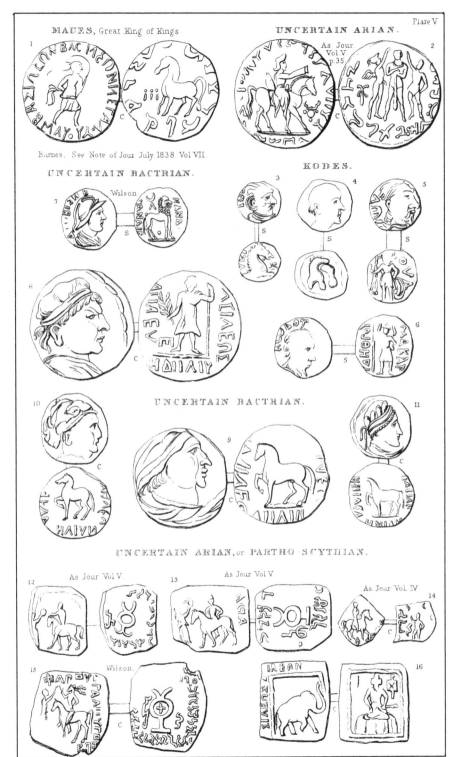

Plate V

MAUES, Great King of Kings

UNCERTAIN ARIAN.

As Jour
Vol.V.
p.35

Barnes. See Note of Jour. July. 1838. Vol VII.

UNCERTAIN BACTRIAN.

KODES.

Wilson

UNCERTAIN BACTRIAN.

UNCERTAIN ARIAN, or PARTHO-SCYTHIAN.

As Jour Vol V.

As Jour Vol V.

As. Jour. Vol. IV.

Wilson.

G.Barclay sc

Plate VII.

AZES, GREAT KING OF KINGS.

SOTERMEGAS, KING OF KINGS.

SOTERMEGAS, KING OF KINGS.

AZILISES, KING OF KINGS, 110, B.C.

J.Prinsep.

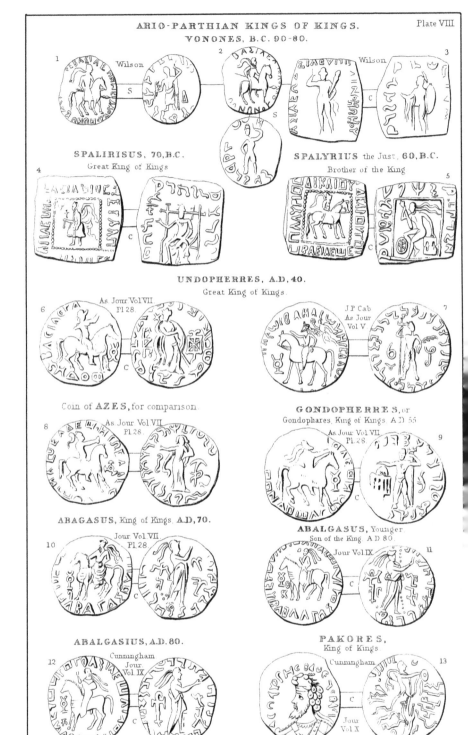

ARIO-PARTHIAN KINGS OF KINGS.
VONONES, B.C. 90-80.

Wilson

Wilson

SPALIRISUS, 70, B.C.
Great King of Kings

SPALYRIUS the Just, 60, B.C.
Brother of the King

UNDOPHERRES, A.D. 40.
Great King of Kings.

As Jour Vol VII
Pl 28.

J P Cab
As Jour
Vol V

Coin of AZES, for comparison.

GONDOPHERRES, or
Gondophares, King of Kings. A.D. 55

As Jour Vol VII
Pl 28.

ABAGASUS, King of Kings. A.D. 70.

ABALGASUS, Younger
Son of the King. A.D. 80.

Jour Vol IX

ABALGASIUS, A.D. 80.

Cunningham
Jour
Vol. IX.

PAKORES,
King of Kings

Cunningham

Jour
Vol X

G. Barclay

Plate VIII

SCYTHIAN & INDO-SCYTHIAN KINGS.
SOTER MEGAS, Great King of Kings, 80-70. B.C.
Nameless

Plate IX

KORANOS ZATHQS KADPHISES.
B.C.10.

KADAPHES CHORANUS.
10, B.C.

KORSO KOZOULO KADPHISES.

OONM KADPHISES,
Great King of Kings A.D. 0

OOEMO KADPHISES,
Great King of Kings A.D. 0

KANERKES, King of Kings
A.D.100.

KENO RANO RAO NANA RAO.
A.D.200.

KANERKES, King of Kings
A.D.100.

G.Barclay sc

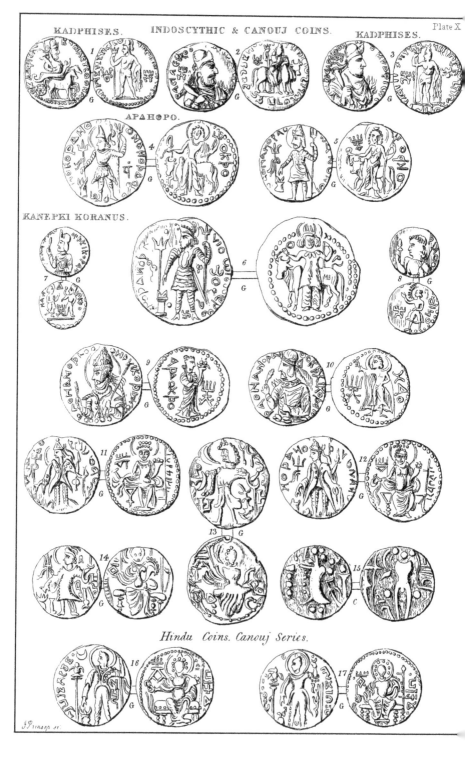

Plate X.

KADPHISES. INDOSCYTHIC & CANOUJ COINS. KADPHISES.

APAHΘPO.

KANEPKI KORANUS.

Hindu Coins. Canouj Series.

J.Prinsep sc.

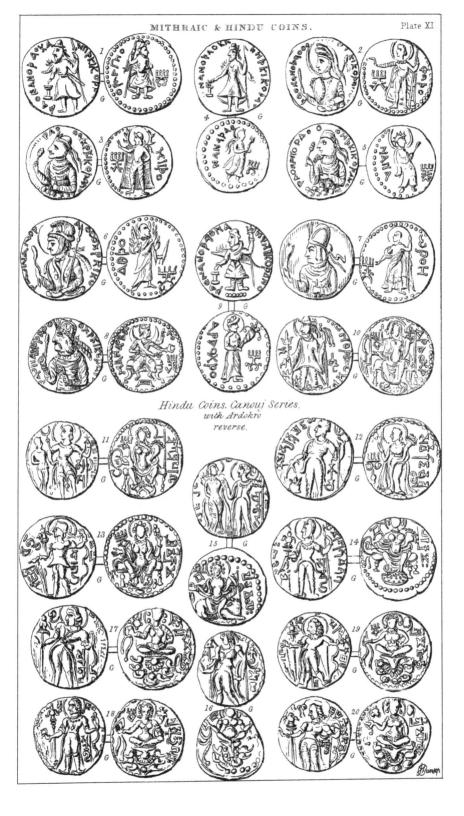

Hindu Coins. Canouj Series.
with Ardokro
reverse.

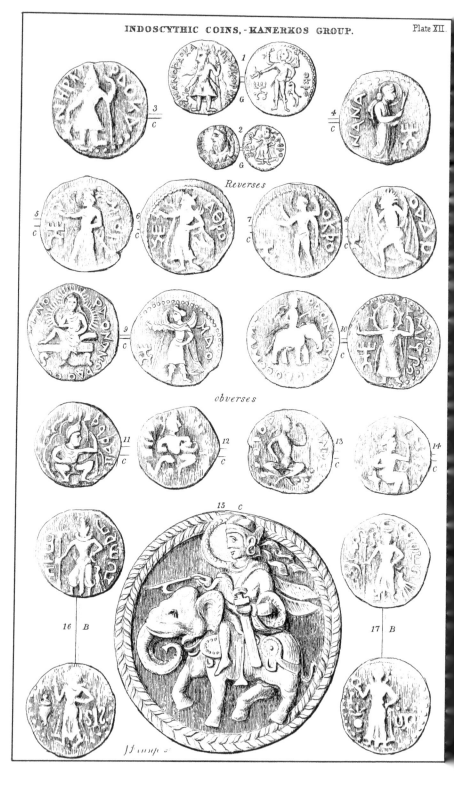

INDOSCYTHIC COINS,—KANERKOS GROUP.

Plate XII.

Plate XIII

Inscriptions in Greek and Pehlavi on Bactrian Coins.

1 ΒΑΣΙΛΕΩΣ ΜΕΓΑΛΟΤ ΕΤΚΡΑΤΙΔΟΤ

2 ΒΑΣΙΛΕΩΣ ΣΩΤΗΡΟΣ ΜΕΝΑΝΔΡΟΤ

3 ΒΑΣΙΛΕΩΣ ΣΩΤΗΡΟΣ ΑΠΟΛΛΟΔΟΤΟΤ

4 ΒΑΣΙΛΕΩΣ ΣΩΤΗΡΟΣ ΕΡΜΑΙΟΤ

5 ΒΑΣΙΛΕΩΣ ΒΑΣΙΛΕΩΝ ΜΕΓΑΛΟΤ ΑΖΟΤ

6 ΒΑΣΙΛΕΩΣ ΒΛΣΙΛΕΩΝ ΜΕΓΑΛΟΤΑΖΙΛΙΣΟΤ

7 ΒΑΣΙΛΕΩΣ ΑΝΙΚΗΤΟΤ ΦΙΛΟΞΕΝΟΤ

8 ΒΑΣΙΛΕΩΣ ΝΙΚΗΦΟΡΟΤ ΑΝΤΙΜΑΧΟΤ

9 ΒΑΣΙΛΕΩΣ ΜΕΓΑΛΟΤ ΟΝΩΝΟΤ

10 ΒΑΣΙΛΕΩΣ ΝΙΚΗΦΟΡΟΤ ΑΝΤΙΑΛΚΙΔΟΤ

11 ΒΑΣΙΛΕΩΣ ΑΝΙΚΗΤΟΤ ΛΥΣΙΟΤ

12 ΒΑΣΙΛΕΩΣ ΣΩΤΗΡΟΣ ΥΝΔΑΦΕΡΡΟΥ

13 ΒΑCΙΛΕΩΣ ΣΤΗΡΟΣ ΣΥ. ΕΡΜΑΙΟΤ

14 ΒΑCΙΛΕΥC ΒΑCΙΛΕΩΝCΩΤΗΡΜΕΓΑC ΟΟΜΝΚ ΑΔΦΙCΗC

15 ....ΚΑΔΑΦΕC......ΧΟΡΑΝΟΥ.............

Titles and Epithets.

16 ΒΑΣΙΛΕΩΣ
Maharajasa

ΜΕΓΑΛΟΤ ΒΑΣΙΛΕΩΣ
Mahatasa   Maharajasa

17 ΒΑΣΙΛΕΩΣ ΒΑΣΙΛΕΩΝ
Rajatirajasa

18 ΣΩΤΗΡΟΣ
Tradatasa

19 ΑΝΙΚΗΤΟΥ
Apatihasa – & Apatihata...

20 ΝΙΚΗΦΟΡΟΤ
Jyatarasa

Names of Princes

21 ΑΠΟΛΛΟΔΟΤΟΥ

22 ΑΝΤΙΑΛΚΙΔΟΥ

23 ΑΝΤΙΜΑΧΟΥ

24 ΑΖΟΥ

25 ΑΖΙΛΙΣΟΥ

26 ΕΤΚΡΑΤΙΔΟΥ

27 ΕΡΜΑΙΟΥ

28 ΜΕΝΑΝΔΡΟΤ

29 ΛΥΣΙΟΥ

30 ΦΙΛΟΞΕΝΟΤ

31 ΟΝΩΝΟΥ

32 ΣΥ ΕΡΜΑΙΟΤ (ΚΑΔΦΙΖΟΤ)

33 ΥΝΔΑΦΕΡΡΟΥ

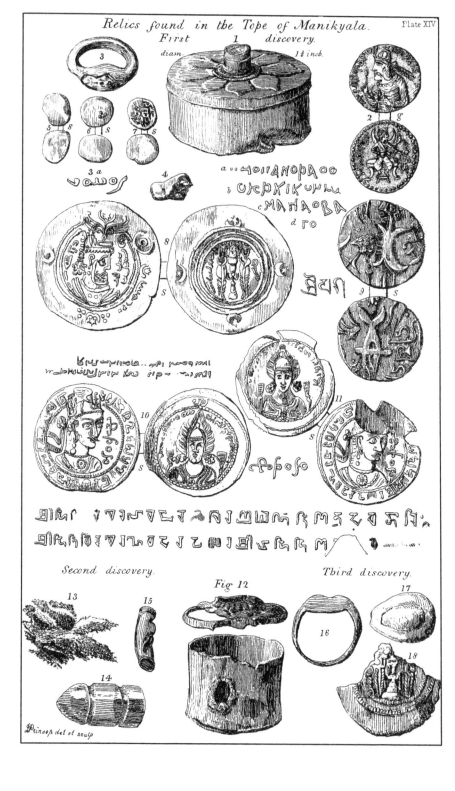

Relics found in the Tope of Manikyala.
First 1 discovery.

diam. 1¼ inch.

Second discovery. Fig 12 Third discovery.

Prinsep del et sculp.

Plate XIV

Relics found in the Tope of Manikyala.

Principal deposit

Plate XV

inscription on brass cylinder.

Characters scratched around a brass cylinder found in a Tope at Jelalabad.

ditto on the lid of the same.

J.Prinsep del et sculp.

FAC-SIMILE of A ARIAN INSCRIPTION FROM MANIKYALA TOPE.

¼ lin. dimensions

Taken by James Prinsep from a wax impression received from Genl. Court.

a.e i au u

ka kai ke ku ki

kha khai khi

ch?

ju?

t ti to tai te tra

th thi thai the

duri da d

da di dai de du

dha

pa pai pu pi pe

fa te fu fra ai?

t bai

w Ψ

ya yi yu

ra re ri tu

la le lda

va ve vi vri

ha hai hi he

sha shria sui sta

sh shi shu

sa se su sta sta?

chh chhu ksha

u

na ne

KAPOORDIGERI Inscription sent by Sir A Burnes. to Jas Prinsep

For EU product safety concerns, contact us at Calle de José Abascal, 56–1°,
28003 Madrid, Spain or eugpsr@cambridge.org.

www.ingramcontent.com/pod-product-compliance
Ingram Content Group UK Ltd.
Pitfield, Milton Keynes, MK11 3LW, UK
UKHW012339130625
459647UK00009B/408